The Freelance Cannabis Writer's Handbook

Leaf Writers Publishing
www.leafwriters.com

First Printing, 2020

Leaf Writers Publishing
www.leafwriters.com

Absorb what is useful, discard what is useless and add what is
specifically your own.
– Bruce Lee

Contents

Introduction

By being able to work remotely from anywhere, freelancers today are leveraging their skills to earn income that's unrestrained by time and place. Today, you can get your taxes done by an accountant in Canada, hire a programmer from the Philippines to build an app, and have your Columbian virtual assistant plan your weekly meals. Technology is constantly and rapidly redefining work— and it's a beautiful thing!

People around the world living very different lives can make a living doing things they couldn't have just a few short years ago. They can specialize in a service of their choice and work remotely any time of day that works for them. There's no commuting, no office politics, no working in the elements, and nobody telling *you* how to build *their* dream.

And it's a win for the people who hire the freelancers too. Why invest in a full-time employee when you can get the job done cheaper and without any long-term commitment or investment in training? That is the question many employers are asking, particularly after the COVID-19 pandemic exposed the liability of having a full time workforce in a physical location. Being light and nimble is a proven way for businesses to get through tough times.

This all makes Freelancing the future of work for many. We're rapidly headed toward a world where much of the 9 to 5 work gives way to more flexible, independent, and increasingly remote employment.

I wanted to become a freelance cannabis writer because I enjoy the physical act of writing and the growing cannabis space seemed like a fun industry to write for. Maybe you feel similarly.

It seemed like the kind of industry where I could create a service business with the kinds of clients I wouldn't totally hate working with. Bovine insemination whitepapers might sell like crazy but I don't think I'd dig writing them. Maybe people in that industry are dope as hell too, but I'll never find out.

So I set out to stake a claim writing for an industry I thought would be chill to write for and decided to start my new business. But I didn't know where to start.

At that point I did what most obsessive entrepreneur types would do— since obsessive is what entrepreneur types often seem to be. I devoured all the info I could find on the subject. Then I digested it, and started to write myself a basic business guide to help me get started. It was super rough but writing it helped me to get my head straight about the whole thing. I hoped it would help the new project run more smoothly.

And that's what the book your reading now started out as— an internal resource I made for myself to help me stay focused with my new freelance business. My attention span is non-existent and I need constant instructions of what to do to keep focused or I'll just get distracted. It was supposed to be my cheat sheet, if you will.

It would have remained as just an internal process document for my new personal business, but at some point I decided to post some of the writing to the "knowledge hub" of the site I built for my freelancing business, leafwriters.com.

Apparently people appreciated what I wrote and that I had shared it. I got some great feedback saying how much the posts helped with their own freelance writing business. That felt amazing. It's always incredible to hear that you helped somebody, and it's also an alarm bell that Mr. Market might have an interest in more of that kind of information.

The surprise positive reception to my terrible writing got my entrepreneur hairs all on end. What if I organized all the tidbits together and polished them up into one less terrible *mega-guide*? Which I did. Which is whatever *this* all is. Thanks for picking it up by the way!

This book covers how to start a freelance cannabis writing business for yourself and land freelance, contract-based assignments. Something this book *doesn't* cover is how to get hired for full-time writing gigs as a staff writer. That's not to say reading this book won't be helpful in landing a full time gig, it's just beyond the scope of this book.

If this book is at all helpful for you, please consider writing an honest review of it on Amazon.com. I'd be immensely grateful. Reviews are hugely important to independently published books like this one. In gratitude for your support, I'd also like to extend you an invitation to be a beta reader for my future books on similar topics. If you're interested in getting free books in exchange for some feedback, please head over to leafwriters.com/beta for details.

How to Use This Guide

This book was written to be flipped through and read in any order that helps you best. Don't feel like you need to read the whole thing page for page in one stretch. You're the wise, self-knowing leader here, my friend.

Lead on.

Part I - Cannabis Writing and You

Do you love reading, writing, and also smoking weed? It's a safe bet you do, since you picked up this book (thanks again for that BTW!).

Well then, grab a writing implement and the strain of your fancy and strap yourself in for the gig of a lifetime. Or perhaps just for a little while. Maybe it's a good side hustle to put a dent in those student loans.

Like with anything else, the only way you're going to know if this job is a good fit for you is to give it a go. You can read all the books you want but you'll never know if you don't give it a shot, right?

When faced with large decisions such as which profession to choose or what to do with the rest of our lives, we lack procedures or rituals. We have no prior experience to draw from to judge the decision and gauge how it's likely to turn out. Unsurprisingly, in such circumstances, we often fall victim to decision paralysis and procrastinate (possibly while high).

The nice thing about freelancing, though, is that it's relatively easy and affordable to give it a go and see how you like it. It's not a gigantic scary commitment. By and large, cannabis industry clients are a chill bunch and for the most part, there's very little that can go wrong from writing about weed.

Perhaps as a child, you had big dreams of becoming a professional writer but somewhere along the way you lost your confidence or lacked the tools to pursue writing as a career. The cannabis gods are looking out for you. Thanks to the digital freelance economy, it is now possible to make a living writing about cannabis with very little risk involved.

We wrote this book to help you understand what it looks like to be a cannabis writer today and figure out for yourself whether this job might be a good fit for you. Let's get started by putting things into perspective.

Why Choose Cannabis Writing

Weed is going mainstream and there are fortunes to be made during the cannabis renaissance. Everywhere you look, people are doing everything they can to get involved in the early days of the much lauded green rush. The feeling is that you've got to move fast or you'll miss the big chance.

We might not all have the resources, personal network, and knowledge to grow, sell, or invest in cannabis— but some of us can write!

The future is shaped by the past, knowledge is transferred through text, and text shapes future perceptions. Heady stuff, but all it means is your work is timeless if you know what you are doing. You're basically a motherfucking time traveling immortal badass. As Winston Churchill once said. *"history will be kind to me. For, I intend to write it myself"*.

The great thing about picking a specific niche is that through your work, you get to learn a lot of things about the subject matter. You go from very general knowledge to specific knowledge in the span of your career. Things get easier. People start to think of you as an expert in your field. What does that make you? An industry professional!

What is Cannabis Writing Exactly?

Writing has a huge effect on the way we view the world. Upton Sinclair's The Jungle made us view poverty and slaughterhouse conditions in a different light, All Quiet On The Western Front introduced us to the horrors of World War I, and so on. But what about when writing portrays the real world or conditions that you are living in?

We are in the midst of a cannabis renaissance and the industry needs people who will shape the way future generations look at cannabis. As a writer you might not always think of yourself as being part of history, but the way we creatively present cannabis use in our culture is absolutely important.

And it's important to keep things positive. Cannabis has enough negative baggage. It doesn't need the oft repeated lazy stoner anachronisms and dreariness.

In the line of duty, you will be hired by clients to do very specific jobs. And you'll be the only one responsible for making sure it gets done by deadline. Consequently, you will need to learn how to work with yourself and focus. In essence, what I'm saying is this is not a run of the mill 9 to 5 kind of job.

If you're used to switching your brain off at the end of the day, being freelance is going to take some getting used to. We will go into specifics in later chapters but what I'm telling you is a freelance cannabis writer is not an employee. Seems really basic, but there's a lot there to get your head around for people who have worked for somebody else their whole life.

What Kinds of Things Will I Get Paid to Write?

Cannabis industry businesses need all different kinds of written content. A few of the most popular writing jobs you'll come across are:

- Ads for television, radio, and on the internet
- Brochures for B2C, B2B sales, and cannabis centered brochures in general
- Content for social media
- Cannabis blog content
- Scripts for salespeople and customer support to follow
- Screenplays for cannabis related movies and shows
- Podcast content
- Youtube content
- Course writing
- Strain descriptions
- Educational content
- Press Releases

- Instructional & technical manuals
- Email sequences
- Product descriptions
- Website copywriting

Write What You Know

In the writing profession, you will hear this term over and over. See, the average marijuana user can tell right away when a writer doesn't really know anything about weed. They want reliable, useful knowledge that's presented in an authentic way by a voice they can relate to. This is a very tough niche to conquer if you don't occasionally indulge in a little reefer.

For that reason, it's really a gig best suited for people who genuinely have personal relationships with the plant. If you don't genuinely enjoy weed, there are probably better topics to consider writing about.

The Demand for Cannabis Writers

Traditionally, we go to school to learn new trades. But cannabis has been illegal for most of our lives. That means that there are very few writers with advanced knowledge about cannabis. But demand dictates supply and demand is on the rise.

You'd have to be living under a rock not to see how quickly the tides of marijuana prohibition are turning these last few years. One after another, countries and states are decriminalizing or fully legalizing cannabis. Not to mention locations with existing medicinal marijuana programs in place. This legislative trend has helped fuel the green rush and has created enormous growth for many growers, distributors, and pot businesses of all kinds that sell physical products to customers. All these cannabis industry brands need support service businesses of all kinds to keep their gears turning and products sold. Marketers, designers, developers, programmers, digital marketing specialists, SEO specialists, and of course, writers. But Does that mean that it's a wise industry to get into long-term?

Despite the usual volatility and stock fluctuations inherent in any new industry, the cannabis market overall has grown remarkably steadily. In a self-perpetuating way, trends of legalization are fueling industry growth and that growth is in turn funding lobbying efforts to further legalization.

Looking forward to 2027 (that's less than 7 years away by the way!) it's predicted that the industry will be worth a jaw-dropping $73.6 billion.

Admittedly, these kinds of predictions make a lot of assumptions and aren't guaranteed to come to fruition. It *is* guaranteed however that enterprising individuals will *always* follow the flow of money into growing markets and to some extent that money will make the industry more and more powerful. As it does, it'll become less and less likely to be swept aside by future prohibitionist legislative changes.

To generate the kind of money that analysts are predicting, the industry needs not only growers and distributors, but supporting entrepreneurs of all kinds who know their trichomes from their terpenes. That's where you come in.

As a writer looking to provide writing services to these kinds of companies you basically have three options. Join an agency, work as a staff writer directly for a business, or become a freelance writer. While there are benefits to joining an agency or being a staff writer for a business, those positions don't offer the same level of flexibility and freedom that working for yourself does.

How Competitive is the Cannabis Freelance Niche?

What's to stop the same oversupply issues that cannabis growers deal with afrom happening with cannabis copywriters and writers? Ultimately nothing. It's totally conceivable that so many people will become marijuana writers that there will be tons of competition. But the great thing about writing is that you can let your writing do the talking for you. You don't have to worry about pricing more competitive than other freelancers — you just need to be a better writer.

If you're genuinely a better writer than most of the competition, clients will see that right away and you'll be able to charge more and get hired more. Buying writing from a freelancer isn't like buying cannabis itself. You can spend $10 on a pre rolled mid-grade joint or you can spend WAY more than that for some huge fancy joint— but they'll both get you high. There's a difference, but either way, you're getting high. With writing on the other hand, you *really* get what you pay for. There's a huge difference between a writer who can barely string two sentences together and somebody who really knows the business and sounds like they know what they're doing. It's noticeable to anybody right away. And clients absolutely know the difference. So dedicating yourself to becoming a good writer and devoting time to improving your craft really does pay off. It'll be the thing that helps get you the jobs instead of your competition.

The gig economy is in full swing right now and more and more people are turning to freelance work to pay the bills. So there will always be lots of competition for writers; probably more each year. It's just something to expect.

But as a specialized cannabis writer, you have an ace up your sleeve!

Instead of being a general run of the mill jack-of-all-trades master-of-none kind of freelancer. You have specialized in a niche that you are truly good at writing about.

Try this. Take a random sample of freelancers. You will notice that freelancers tend to come in two varieties. We have 'the generalists' who work on different types of projects for different industries and we have the more specialized freelancers who only work within a particular niche. Think medical writers, wellness podcast writers, food blog writers, and on and on.

Choosing a particular niche tells your clients that you are focused and know your market. If I'm a writer who specializes in erotic vampire billionaire romance, you can bet that i'll know everything there is to know about that niche. I must - because of all the infinite things there are to write about, I've chosen to specialize in this one thing.

Cannabis Writing and You

If you're interested in applying your writing skills to writing about weed, most would probably agree it's important you use it too. At least occasionally. Sure you can write about anything theoretically, but it's going to be tough to come across as authentic if you don't really get high now and then. This disclaimer probably wasn't needed. If you gravitated towards wanting to write about pot you most likely enjoy it.

As a writer, you probably also carry around a notepad and pen or some kind of note taking apparatus. Maybe you use your phone for notes or email yourself. If you don't carry around something to write with wherever you go, I'd like to strongly impress upon you the potential benefit this can have on your productivity. It's useful, because you never know when you're going to think of some amazing way to say something. And if you don't write it down there's pretty much *zero* chance you'll remember it. Especially if you were stoned when you thought of that great idea. Great writing ideas can happen anywhere, be it in the bathroom or even while having cannabis tea with your sweet grandmama. She'll be folding those tea towels and laughing to herself for hours, let's move on.

Pros and Cons of Writing for the Cannabis Industry

We all have reasons why we choose the careers we choose. If you are going to choose writing as a full-time job, it's important to find joy in the thing that puts food on the table. Or at least not total disdain.

Does writing everyday cause you pain? Does it feel like a chore? Or do you enjoy it despite the crampy fingers, hunched back and hours and hours spent behind a screen?

Yes, writing is hard work, but, if you enjoy it, you are no longer at work!

For me, writing doesn't feel like work. It's pleasant. Sometimes it's more pleasant than other times but in general it's an enjoyable activity. It's a pretty posh gig compared to a whole lot of jobs.

Not everybody feels like that. To some people having to write something is as fun as going to the dentist. But if you do enjoy writing, there are plenty of worse things to write about than a magical plant.

When Freelance Cannabis Writing is an Amazing Gig

What benefits are we talking about?

- Autonomy: You won't have to answer to anyone — you operate on your terms.
- Flexibility of location: Good internet speed, a laptop or tablet. That's all you need.
- Freedom to choose: You decide what jobs to apply and which ones to ignore.
- No office politics: You are not competing with anyone; the corner office is already yours.
- Earn beyond geographic borders: You're not limited by your country or region.
- A chance to experiment with your craft and better yourself.
- Freedom, no commute, income control.

When Freelance Writing Can Be The Worst Thing Ever

Let's dig into the less endearing parts about writing about weed for a living. The things that make you want to give it up and try something else. Real talk. Some problems that might make you want to hang your keyboard and call it quits are:

- Clients who make vague requests or are unsure of what their needs are.
- Poor communication and unreliable clients.
- Low payment, late payment, and finding a continuous flow of work.
- Vague requests.
- Not everyone will understand and support your work.

- It can get lonely working for yourself.
- Difficult clients.
- Taxes! Good god, taxes.

Not to mention, sending proposals regularly can be tedious, getting reviews can be problematic and at first before you build a solid enough reputation you will have to work for pennies. You might be thinking. *"with all that, who'd want to be a freelancer?"*.

It's a valid question. But there can be tough days to just about any job. Personally, I'd just feel way better working 80 hours a week building my own dream than 40 hours building somebody else's dream every week of my life. If you don't feel that way, a job can be a lot less stress and potentially more consistent money than freelancing.

How do I Know I'll Be Any Good at This?

Remember here those words of wisdom your mom (probably) told you: "You'll never know if you don't try!".

If you have the following skills, you will without a doubt crush cannabis freelance writing:

- Good grammar, spelling, and attention to detail.
- You love reading/avid reader (helps with grammar, sentence structure...)
- Decent Editing skills
- Networking and marketing skills
- Strong research skills
- Solid understanding of SEO
- Ability to remain focused

Questions to Consider

In certain ways, freelancer's lives aren't much different from the nomadic hunter gatherer lives our ancestors once had. Except now instead of roaming the land in search of sustenance, freelancers spend their days hunched over a laptop moving from project to project. Constantly on the hunt for a fresh new employer. The prey is out there waiting, but you've got to ask yourself:

- Can you handle rejection?
- Do you have the experience to undertake the gargantuan task ahead?
- Do you know when to say yes and when to say NO?
- Are you confident enough to ask to be paid what you are worth?
- Are you willing to give up the security of a paycheck?
- How good are you with finances?

These questions not only open up a can of worms and awkward realizations, but they also force you to question yourself on several levels. Here are a few other questions to ask yourself before you get started freelancing.

1. What Is My Current Financial Situation?
It's ideal to have some cash reserves on hand to get started, since you won't start getting paid until you nab your first clients and complete their jobs.

Before you give up your day job, you must first figure out how you are going to survive for at least the next three months. There is no shame in moving back home or choosing to work part-time until you start bringing in more regular pay from jobs. What matters is setting your foundation right so you're set to succeed. More important than how much cash you have saved, is that you possess some key traits to guide you.

Here are a few key traits you'll need to have to succeed freelance writing:

- **Well thought out action:** Stop dreaming and start applying for jobs.
- **The drive to improve:** Today I know some things, tomorrow I will learn more.
- **Resiliency:** You will fail, the important question is, are you willing to get back up?
- **Consistency:** You must be consistent in your work, hustle and brand building.

2. Do I have the mental and physical capacity to deliver?

If you have never written as your primary source of income, it might seem like pretty easy work. And it is, relatively speaking. But once you start, the 'devil' can sometimes emerge.

- You start noticing how lonely you are.
- Lack of proper posture causes back pain, eye strain, and pain in places you never realized you had.
- The pressure of working multiple jobs threatens to squeeze the life out of you.

All these things drain your energies, physically and emotionally. So, it's important to self-access and work on any personal weaknesses. Also, make sure to reassure yourself you're strong enough to get through this. How we speak to ourselves has a big effect on what we can achieve.

3. Have you conquered the imposter syndrome?

Do I deserve to charge what I'm charging per hour? Is my work good enough for someone to pay for? Do I even look like I know what I'm doing? These questions represent a part of your psyche that's constantly telling you *"you are not good enough!"*.

Imposter syndrome is the proverbial iceberg that sinks many freelance careers. It is essentially you doubting your skills. How can you be confident if your mind is working against your ambitions?

Self-doubt is inevitable, however, freeing yourself from it liberates you from negative thinking.

A few ways to overcome self-doubt are:

- Stop dwelling on past mistakes or jobs that didn't go right.
- Set reachable goals and only bite what you can chew.
- When feeling overwhelmed, breathe through it.
- Stop trying to make everyone else happy. That priority should only be reserved for well-paying clients.
- Surround yourself with positive people, not people who trivialize what you do.

The Benefits of Writing For Specialized Markets

The awesome thing about niche topics like cannabis is you don't need years and years of experience. The only thing you need is to understand your client's business.

To that end, you can research the business or simply ask questions. Think about it, if you specialize in cannabis writing. Will you know about every single topic in the cannabis industry from the get go? Heck no!

But you can look at the client's website, you can ask him or her for samples and you can use available information to acquaint yourself with the task at hand. The idea is to be good at filling knowledge gaps. Yes, experience matters too, but don't let your lack of it keep you from applying for your first jobs.

Writing Niches Within The Cannabis Industry

Although it's totally fine to write as a generalist in the cannabis industry, you may eventually decide that you prefer to specialize in a particular niche within the cannabis space.

For instance, you might really be personally motivated to write about the financial side of the cannabis industry or maybe on legal or political topics. Maybe the healing aspects of CBD are something you are passionate about and you may decide to commit to that exclusively. Perhaps you really like writing medically oriented content. If you're writing about an aspect of the plant that you personally connect with, you'll be much more likely to do an amazing job writing. The more you are able to establish yourself as a voice of trust and authority in your area of expertise, the more business will flow to you.

Pay can vary widely between different segments of the cannabis writing industry, so you will most likely want to investigate what jobs pay in different niches that appeal to you. Sometimes you may find that higher paying jobs will require specialized education— but not always.

A few of the many writing niches in the cannabis sector include:

- Resume writing: Write resumes for people looking for jobs in the cannabis space.
- Grant writer: Specializes in creating compelling grant proposals for organizations or individuals.
- Copywriter: Write text or content for marketing purposes or to reach target audiences.
- Report writer: Analyze, draft and or write reports
- Technical writer: Help others understand technical information easily.
- Medical writer: Use your medical expertise to write health and wellness pieces.
- Writer for cannabis-related shows: Screenplays, etc.
- Political cannabis writer
- Legal cannabis writer
- Recipe Producer and writer for cannabis cooking

There are so many different types of sub-niches within the bigger niche of cannabis writing that it's impossible to list them all here. Who knows, maybe a brand is making an Indiegogo campaign for their new CBD line for hamsters and needs a video script. You can be hired to write literally anything related to cannabis.

This tactic of selecting a smaller subcategory or sub-niche is often referred to as "niching down". By niching down into a sub-niche of the larger cannabis space, you'll have less direct competition to worry about and you'll have an easier time tracking down potential clients within your smaller industry segment.

The downside, of course, is that you'll have to acquire highly specialized knowledge that can take a while to attain. This knowledge could require considerable education and may take time to acquire.

Making a Life, Not Just a Living

Today, more than one in three American workers freelances either as a side hustle or as a full-time job.

Pay is the first requirement for any type of job. Almost as important yet much less frequently talked about, is that a job should feel like it's taking you somewhere. By that I mean, your work should give you purpose or meaning.

There's nothing to lose by giving freelance writing a go. Give it a try and see if it's something that speaks to you.

In the next chapter, we'll cover the basics of freelance writing and how to actually begin finding your first clients. Don't worry if you don't have a portfolio yet— there's a technique I'll show you to get your first clients without one.

Part II - Getting Started Freelancing

Before we dive in, a little mood setting to get in the right headspace. You want to start this business on the right foot, right?

If you're serious about wanting to earn a living writing, or serious about any goal whatsoever— it's important to come into it with the right attitude. It may seem a little obvious, but if you're not starting this venture from a good place it's not going to go anywhere. It's that way with anything. Things started well have a greater propensity to turn out well. Or, as Plato put it, "The beginning is the most important part of the work"

Approach freelancing as an exciting adventure rather than a mundane quest to pay bills and you'll have a way easier time making a go of it.

I really believe being in business for yourself can help you know yourself better and help your life to run more smoothly. It's done that for me. Your business will have its ups and downs, sure. Overall though, you'll be more self-reliant, confident, and happy— since you'll have a definite goal. Goals are something that positively correlate with happiness for most people. They give us purpose, and something to strive for.

So what I'm saying is, it's not a one way street— your healthy and happy life will help your business grow and your business will nurture your life.

Commit Yourself To Success

Making a living freelance writing is not about talent, it's about dedicating yourself to something and getting good at it! Writing is a noble craft and like all crafts, it's meant to be practiced and honed.

Another trait a lot of entrepreneurial types seem to have is jumping around from idea to idea without really seeing any of them through. Sound like you? I know it's like me. Can you stick it out and see this freelancing thing through when things get tough?

Steve Jobs nailed it when it said:

"People think focus means saying yes to the thing you've got to focus on. But that's not what it means at all. It means saying no to the hundred other good ideas that there are. You have to pick carefully. I'm actually as proud of the things we haven't done as the things I have done."

The truth is, the start of a new business is the honeymoon phase. All your feel-good hormones are in full effect and everything is looking new and beautiful. Optimism is high. Maybe you'll be able to quit your day job! At this early stage it doesn't feel much like work at all.

After a while though, it's easy for it to become a grind just like any work can at times. Once you start writing more, it's easy for the pressures of the job to start getting to you.

I'm talking late nights, painful fingers, headaches, eye strain, pressure to deliver, pressure to find jobs, rejections, revisions, etc.

These pressures can quickly make you want to give in to laziness and give up. Why do something so unpleasant when you can get stoned and binge watch some Netflix?

But you must overcome— be the leader that *you* need *you* to be!

You're probably sick of hearing Thomas Edison saying it, but it's a fact: "Opportunity is missed by most people because it is dressed in overalls and looks like work." But as important as it is to commit and see it through the grind to get to success, that's not even the biggest problem for most people. The biggest issue is just sitting down and typing out that first word. It's just putting yourself out there and getting started.

Once you get past that and start something and develop the right frame of mind for the task at hand, then everything else can flow. You've taken that big scary first step so you can start to let loose and get to know your own personal working preferences. Things like what schedule works best, what types of projects you prefer, how you reward yourself for your successes, etc.

Reasons Why Greenhorn Writers Quit

- You thought that writing was easier than it is
- Inability to handle bad reviews or rejection
- You assume that your writing is perfect
- Impatience
- Low pay or not making enough money
- Expecting immediate success
- Burnout from having to write daily
- Impostor syndrome
- Bad clients
- Fear of Failure

What You Need To Get Started

Writing is a pretty lean business in terms of startup requirements. You can honestly get by with a laptop and a reliable internet connection. Beyond that, most other tools you'll use on a daily basis will be software-based and can be had entirely for free.

Here are a few things you'll want to have to get started.

- A good internet connection and a computer.
- Video chat or messaging services such as Zoom or Skype.
- To-do list to keep you organized.
- Cloud-based document storage such as Dropbox or Google Drive.
- Time tracking tool (sites like Upwork provide this type of software).
- An accounting system to keep track of your finances.
- A good chair. I cannot fully stress the importance of a good chair.

Also, go easy on the coffee. It makes you drowsy once the effects start wearing off.

Choosing Where to Work

This may seem like a fluffy topic, but I strongly believe that it's important where you write. Sure, you should be able to work under any circumstances— but that will come later. In the beginning it's all about removing as many success obstacles as possible. Treat yourself well so that you can perform to the best of your abilities. This includes working in a place where you can feel productive and happy.

Working from home has its perks. but it also has some serious downsides such as boredom, loneliness, lack of physical separation between work and life, and so on. The list of drawbacks is high, as anyone who has worked remotely can tell you.

Things get particularly tricky if you've got young kids home when you're trying to get projects done on schedule. But even with all this, working from home is absolutely amazing. The flexibility of working from home far outweighs the drawbacks. Just the fact that you won't have to commute is such a game changer. Commuting wastes huge amounts of your time and money— and it almost certainly adds considerably to your stress.

Coworking spaces are another option that can be fantastic for networking and getting out of the house. They will cost you money, so in the beginning It's probably best to steer clear of these and keep your expenses low.

Google Docs for Writers

Google Docs is an awesome, word processor that's cross-platform, mobile, and available for any Google user to use for free. Which is a price that writers like to pay. Google Docs is a great alternative to Microsoft Word, and has way more potential that many people (myself included) may have first realized. If you're unfamiliar with Google's suite of tools, you'll quickly find the mobile apps and collaboration options are very useful. If you lose your internet connection, or you want to turn it off for a while, you can use Google Docs in offline mode, and it'll sync as soon as you regain your connection.

Some of Google Docs' lesser-known features are very valuable as well. In particular, Google Docs' Add-Ons are handy little extensions that can improve your workflow and expand the features of the word processor far beyond Word or similar applications.

Recommended Google Docs Add-Ons For Writers

If you do decide to use Google Docs, here are a few productivity Add-Ons that are extremely helpful for writers. I don't have any connection to the developers who made these and I'm *mostly* not going to mention any specific makers. There are lots of different Docs Add-On options available totally for free. Google it. Some of my favorites are:

- THESAURUS - Super useful for any writer. Unless of course you go by Stephen King's advice that "Any word you have to hunt for in a thesaurus is the wrong word. There are no exceptions to this rule.".
- MIND MEISTER – turns a list into a simple (static) mind-map. I like making lists and mind-maps, so I use this one quite a bit.
- CONDITIONAL TEXT HIGHLIGHTER – Set up rules for conditional highlighting! You might use this to keep an eye out for certain words that you misuse, misspell, etc.
- BETTER WORD COUNT – A live wordcount that lives in your sidebar. It will only be visible to you, not anyone viewing your document, but it's still easier to access than Tools > Word count.
- SCREENPLAY FORMATTER – Pretty self-explanatory!
- TRACK MY WORDS – Tracks the number of words you write per minute and displays it in a sidebar.
- DOC TOOLS – Includes some useful extra formatting tools. Very helpful if you need various styles of highlighting, capitalization, etc.
- DISTRACTION FREE MODE – This extension adds a "distraction free" button to Google Docs with 3 color options to pick from.

Recommended Chrome Extensions for Writers

Just like you can with Docs, you can build onto the capability of the Chrome Web browser by making use of Chrome Extensions. The Chrome web store is excellent and you can find extensions there to do just about anything inside your browser. Here are a few that are great for writers:

- DARK READER - You'll need your eyes to write, so keep the screen dark to reduce strain on your eyes. Formerly used mostly by programmers, dark mode has become more common over the years. At the time of writing Docs still lacked a dark mode, so this is a great workaround for now.
- TEXT TO SPEECH VOICE READER - Read your writing to you so you can hear mistakes. It's like having an audiobook of your own writing! You can even have it read in the seductive voice of the opposite sex. Ooh la la!
- NOISLI - This Chrome extension helps block unwanted background noise. Mix different sounds and create your perfect sound environment to work and relax.
- SITE BLOCKERS - Block distracting sites for a period of time you specify. You know the kinds of sites.

Naming Your Brand

The first thing you will have to do is decide what to name your business. I'm not talking about legal business structures like LLC or S-Corps or anything like that— that's something to discuss with your accountant since it will depend on your individual circumstances.

There are two ways to go about naming your new freelance baby. You can use your own name or you can use a fictitious name (AKA Doing Business As, or DBA).

Each option has several considerations that you need to take into account. Conceivably, you might decide you want to sell your business at some point. In this instance, it is wise to go with a fictitious name, why?

Because if the brand has your name it will likely be too tied to you as an individual. It would likely be really tough for a new owner to operate it without you, the namesake, at the helm.

On the other hand, if you go with a fictitious name, you can gradually build up scalable processes and even outsource your actual writing to other freelancers. If you create a business like this that can function autonomously and show consistent income, potential buyers will be all over it. Maybe you never want to sell your business— but wouldn't it be nice to have the option just in case?

On the other hand, using your real name has some great strengths in that it builds a reputation around you, the individual, and your personal brand. Establishing yourself as the brand builds authority and credibility and will allow you to command top rates. Your business looks and feels more personal and it can make it easier to find you on the internet.

Ultimately it's more important to just pick a name (or use your own) and get started. Overthinking things will only waste time. Weigh the pros and cons of each and decide which will work best for your style.

Should I Freelance Full-Time or Part-Time?

Everybody's circumstances are different but I can tell you this: If you have a day job right now, start writing as a side hustle first before you quit. Get to know the trade and when you are confident enough and bringing in good money, then by all means quit!

This brings up another issue. Remember, in freelancing there is no guaranteed weekly paycheck. That seems obvious, but it takes some getting used to for anybody who's only worked for others their whole life.

As a freelance writer you are essentially an independent contractor. That means that when one job is finished, you move to another.

Sometimes you will find it easy to get a new job and sometimes you will spend days or even months not working. Some of it comes down to how well you market yourself and search out opportunities, but some things are out of your control as a loan freelancer. The economy could tank, federal cannabis regulatory changes could complicate things— anything could happen. You won't get laid off, but you could find yourself struggling to find regular clients.

For that reason, seasoned writers recommend that you save enough money to last you *at least* three months. Ideally more.

Additionally, Don't just take jobs without any forethought, take ones that guarantee food on the table even when work is hard to find. Do the math, figure out how much you need to pay bills and other expenses. Also, factor in the platform fees in your rates.

The Pricing Debate: Hourly Rates vs. Flat Project Pricing

Flat rate billing and hourly rate billing each have their own pros and cons. Neither is perfect all the time and some jobs will be better suited for one billing method over the other. Learning to choose between the two for given jobs is just something freelancers have to deal with and develop a personal feel for.

No two jobs are alike and no two freelancers are alike, but here are some pros and cons of each method to help you out:

Setting Your Rates By The Hour

Hourly rates are popular with some clients and do offer the freelancer some benefits as well. For one thing, you'll never get stuck doing more work on a project than you bargained for initially. You'll always get paid for your time. If you charge a flat rate for a project and finish it under deadline and then your client wants revisions, it's much harder to negotiate any sort of rate increase. Hourly on the other hand, your client is contractually obligated to reimburse you for every minute you devote to their project.

Hourly rates are nice and simple too. Every hour of work you complete, you're entitled to a set quantity of payment. Easy. If you clients think your rate is reasonable, they may select you for their project.

It's totally fine to have different hourly rates depending on the task at hand. For example, you may charge twice as much per hour for work on writing short product descriptions as you do to write longform whitepapers.

Lastly, since lots of professions and industries commonly bill by the hour (eg. attorneys, designers, masseuses, etc.) people are already very familiar with the process. They'll also be able to get an idea of the value of your work, relative to the sorts of hourly rates they pay these other service providers.

Why I Hate Setting Rates By The Hour

My big issue with hourly freelance work is that it's way more difficult to get paid more. If you can produce quality work in a short amount of time, it shouldn't mean that you have to be paid a smaller amount.

If you're working hourly and are super efficient and can work quicker than the competition you're not going to get paid more. Counterintuitively, working quicker amounts to less money for an hourly worker. So you're basically disincentivized from working quickly and efficiently— putting your interests directly against the interests of your clients, in a way.

Assume that you can write 1,000 words in one hour. If you are getting paid $15 per hour, it means that you are only taking $15 home (even less after fees). On the other hand, if you charge $45 per 1,000 words you get to walk away with more. In this instance, you're leaving money on the table by working by the hour.

All other things being equal, I would much prefer to charge clients a flat per-project rate. If I work fast and reliably it's like me getting a bonus compared to an hourly rate. So even though I may consider whether a particular job is worth the time in hourly terms, the prices I quote to my clients will always be project-based.

There are some drawbacks to doing things this way, however. You'll need to be able to estimate how much time a project will take you and turn it into a quote. If your estimate isn't accurate and you wind up taking longer than you thought, there isn't a whole lot you can do about it. Client's won't be very excited to hear that you underestimated the complexity of a job and need more money. You agreed to the price after-all, it's not like they're to blame.

If you're charging clients on a per-project basis, you're paid for the individual article (or whatever it is) and don't have to worry about what constitutes a work hour. You'll be paid for what you actually deliver, which makes it nice and simple. There's no worrying about keeping track of hours, so it also makes it considerably easier to switch back and forth between projects. Something I personally like to do.

Charging By The Word

On freelance sites you'll occasionally have clients asking for project quotes on a per-word basis. There are however some potential problems to consider when charging by the word.

Charging by the word might be something the client is doing to stay under budget. To keep you from going over budget, clients might restrict your word count on articles. This could be a problem if you have a hard time doing justice to the topic with so few words.

If you're paid for each word and *don't* have a restriction on word count, it'll be very tempting to just phone it in with some fluffy filler material. You should of course never do such a thing if you value your reputation, but it's a temptation to keep in mind all the same.

Maybe there's a job that you're being paid for based on final word count. Say you wrote an amazing 5,000 word article but after edits from the client it only turned out to be 4,000 words. You may only be paid on the final word count of 4,000 words and not get anything for those removed 1,000.

Beware of these sorts of issues whenever you're working on a per-word basis and get a written contract between you and the client so expectations are clear on both sides.

The Importance of Clear Communication

Whichever billing method you wind up going with for a project, make sure that both parties (that is, you and your client), are always on the same page. There's absolutely no substitute for clear communication and clear expectations between you and the client.

To Keep yourself safe, always insist on having documentation for as much communication as possible. This might even include recording video calls— just make sure they're aware you're recording!

Documenting all communications will save your ass time and time again should there be any disagreements later on about what the project expectations were. Similarly, be aware that contracts may be advisable for more complicated freelance jobs. Nobody loves reading and writing and signing contracts, but if they help you get paid fairly for your work they can be invaluable.

Where Do I Find my First Client?

To a client, any writer presents some risk. New writers, however, are among the riskiest of all. New freelance writers generally don't have any client testimonials or much portfolio material. A client will fear that new writers won't get the job done right, or worse, that they won't deliver anything at all. They'll worry that'll just waste their time and they'll have to pay to have the work done by somebody else.

On freelancing sites like Upwork, clients will oftentimes rule out new freelancers without even checking their profile out, because they're just too unproven— there's too much risk they won't deliver. That $0 under previous earnings is a giant red flag so it's important to show some earnings as fast as you can. The important question here is, if nobody wants to work with newbs with no feedback or portfolio, how do you land your first client?

To get hired, you must get noticed first. When you're first getting started, it's going to be really hard to get clients to passively notice you. You need to be the one that's actively seeking them out. After a while, you'll hopefully start to get some repeat clients and some new clients that found out about you from your old clients (word of mouth). If all goes as planned, you won't need to search out clients forever - they'll eventually seek you out.

Your best bet in the beginning is to hit the clients where you know they are— freelance marketplaces like Upwork and Fiverr. You'll also find them on more writer-focused content marketplaces such as Text Broker or iWriter. Although there are tons of freelancing sites, we're focusing on Upwork here just because it's the biggest and most well known.

What Types of Jobs Should I Look For?

For new writers I recommend shooting for:

- Jobs that are small enough to complete within a few hours or days (don't bite more than you can chew).
- Work that doesn't require special or technical knowledge that you don't possess and can't quickly learn.
- Clients who offer detailed descriptions of what they want.

Getting Your Freelancer Profile Set Up on Upwork

Because it's by far the biggest freelancing platform, we're going to focus on Upwork. You can, and most likely should, diversify and set up accounts on other platforms. After you've signed up for an account, you're going to want to fill out your profile page.

First, knock out the basics:

- Get a good title for the services you offer.
- Write a good overview.
- Add links to any social media accounts
- Upload an introduction video if possible— it doesn't have to be amazing.
- If you have any testimonials or reviews from previous clients, include them in your profile.
- Use every part of your profile to showcase your skills and experience around the subject matter.
- Select a professional, but happy, profile picture
- Use the overview section to showcase your related expertise
- List your certifications if you have any
- Include your employment, education history, and other relevant experiences

The point is, make your profile stand out even before you start applying for jobs, because ultimately you're selling them on you.

Profile Tip 1: Learn From The Best

An easy way to quickly build a solid profile that will get you noticed is by learning what has worked for other successful users on the platform. That way you can model your profile partially on theirs. We're not trying to copy any wording or anything like that, but just to get a general feel for what seems to work.

Check out some freelancer profiles on Upwork that have the highest earnings and ratings. You want to spy on the top talent so that you can get pointers on how to set yourself up for success on the platform. Be on the lookout for things like:

- The overall layout and look of their profile, including photo
- Any marketing strategies they use
- What they talk about in their bio
- The niche they focus on, if there is one
- Whether they mostly charge hourly or per-project
- Previous reviews from clients. What did the client like best?
- What they include in their portfolio
- Any personal policies or working methods

Profile Tip 2: Make it Stand Out

No one likes boring! Use words, images, reports, videos or anything else that will make your profile not boring or generic. I have found lots of success using snippets or excerpts from my work, screenshots, client testimonials, results, case studies and samples of my previous work.

Profile Tip 3: Don't Forget Your Profile SEO

Your goal as a cannabis-focused writer is to pop up on 'Suggested Freelancers' or high in search results anytime cannabis, marijuana, weed or any variation of these words is used. Your profile on Upwork or any other similar site will benefit from proper keyword usage, profile completeness, skill tags, profile visibility, English level, and client recommendations. Make sure you fill out as much as possible.

Landing Clients Without Experience or a Portfolio

I know that to new freelancers with no portfolio or earnings to show, landing a client feels like an impossible task. But it's not. Every successful freelancer started there at some point, myself included. It seems daunting. You're looking through job postings and almost all of them want to see samples of previous writing. The truth is though, even the most experienced writers rarely have portfolio material that will apply for *every* scenario.

There's a very simple approach that will allow you to land your first few clients without having any prior experience or any work to show. You'll be just the writer of your clients dreams and you'll acquire those clients while at the same time building up your portfolio naturally. It's essentially a minimum viable portfolio. Let's dig into how it works.

The Minimum Viable Portfolio Technique (and Why it Works)

The basic premise of this technique is to create a portfolio that requires the least amount of work possible to get you a job. Why spend all your time writing random fake portfolio material on a random topic, when it may never be appropriate to submit to any real clients?

The beauty of this minimum viable portfolio method is that you are creating very small writing samples written specifically to appeal to the needs of individual clients. There is a very simple reason why this approach is such a great way to enter into the freelance writing market— it helps you build up skills gradually and you get paid while learning.

In essence, it is learning as you go. Instead of spending nights tirelessly reading writing advice, working on portfolio material that won't match real client needs, or watching instructional YouTube videos. You learn, earn, and build skills as you progress.

From Newbie to Hired In Three Simple Steps

Step 1: Go Where The Paying Clients Are

Freelance marketplace sites such as Upwork are the most direct route for new writers to connect with clients. You'll be able to search through a wide selection of different kinds of writing work— some of which will hopefully be suitable for this technique.

First, start looking through job postings by searching for keywords such as cannabis, marijuana, hemp, cbd, thc, etc. As mentioned, you want to pick only jobs that are very detailed and give clear descriptions of what you're expected to deliver and when you're expected to deliver it. You do not want to be shooting in the dark here with what the client wants. The unfortunate reality is that a lot of clients don't really know what they want— so naturally they'll be very tough to please. Avoid mushy sounding projects without definite requirements at all costs.

Step 2: Be Everything The Client Is Looking For

Client's are people, just like you. They've got a job they need done and they're trying to find the best person for that job. It's up to you to convince them that's you.

Clients will avoid spammy proposals, obvious canned messages that aren't on-topic, and anything with glaring spelling or grammatical errors. They're looking for writers. Nobody wants to hire writers that can't even spell. They're way more likely to pick freelancers who quote within the budget, show an earnest interest, communicate professionally, and have an on-topic writing sample.

You want to instill confidence in the potential client by showing them writing you did that's as close as possible to the sort of writing they're looking for. You want them to read your writing and think, "Wow, this one's perfect! And they're focused on writing about weed too so hey, they must know their stuff, right? Let's go with them.". You want them so confident in you that they can't wait to click that hire button and get things rolling.

While you want to craft a writing sample that's very close to the clients actual topic, it's crucially important to not write something that's so good that the client can just use it as-is. You don't want them to be tempted to not pay you. In my experience this isn't likely to ever happen— but it's something to be aware of nonetheless.

To avoid the client using the sample and not paying you, the writing needs to be very similar to what the job is calling for, but different enough to not be usable as-is. For example, if the client wants an article written about "Top 10 Weed Friendly Hotels In Vancouver", you might show them an article you wrote that's something like, "The 8 Top Cannabis Cafes to Check Out In Los Angeles". Both articles may wind up having a lot in common, but they're different enough so that an unscrupulous client can't use it without paying.

The problem with most newbie freelance writers is they focus on the result. They don't want to do anything for free, even if it leads to paid jobs. But the thing is, if you created a portfolio just to show clients, you'd be writing that for free anyway. With this method, there's at least a reasonable chance that the portfolio material you write may get you hired. You're marketing yourself, plain and simple.

It's important to also acknowledge the fact that it's not about you. It's about your client's needs. They're your new boss, in a way. Fortunately, they're also a boss you can fire if things turn ugly.

The question then becomes how do I meet the needs of this client? How do I show potential clients that I am the best writer they could possibly ask for to do this job? In addition to creating that portfolio piece just for the client, it's a good idea to also customize your profile to emphasize what makes you a great fit for this particular job. The same way you would do with a resume— you want the client to visualize you in the role they're looking to fill. Tweak your profile so that it's not only specific to your niche, but also stands out to that client you're trying to win over.

So you've spruced up your profile and created a writing sample that's perfectly tailored just for the client you're trying to win over. You're almost ready to roll. One last thing. Make sure to put your best foot forward in terms of communication etiquette. Any time you speak with the client, make sure your messages are clear, friendly, enthusiastic, and most importantly— FAST. You need to respond to messages quickly and be upbeat because nobody wants to wait and nobody wants to work with somebody who is going to kill the mood of the project.

Step 3: Overdeliver and Stack Up The Good Reviews

From experience I can tell you that the great thing about this method is that you don't have to rely on it for very long. The biggest benefit of using this technique is that as you write more samples and put them in your portfolio, your work starts speaking for itself and your portfolio grows almost without you noticing it.

Additional Tips For Building Your Portfolio

As your portfolio grows, make sure you're constantly updating it in each place that you post it. Here are a few tips to help your portfolio live its best life.

Tell A Story For Each Service Your Provide

Keep your best work front and center, and along with it describe not only the service but also the skills you employed when writing it. If you are multitalented, upload multiple portfolio items showcasing your range of skills in, let's say, blogging, website copywriting, screenplays, etc.

Provide Background Info On Each Portfolio Item

After writing and posting a portfolio item, don't just wait for the magic to happen. Instead, explain the project, how you tackled the problem, the main task or deliverables, the skills and tools you used, and anything else that will help better understand the work you did.

Update Your Portfolio Regularly to Reflect New Skills

Today you know much more than you did last year, so why not tell clients about your newly acquired skills? This is especially important if you acquire any certifications or accolades of any kind that clients will respect.

Keep Your Profile Current With Trends

It's important to keep track of market trends in cannabis writing overall so that you can fine tune your portfolio to emphasize what's trending at the moment. Revamp old project descriptions to call out the expertise and skills that are most in-demand at the moment.

Don't Put All Your Eggs in One Basket

At this point, you've created your Upwork profile and you're on your way to wowing your first clients. Alright alright! High five! Take a sec to be proud of yourself. But what happens if Upwork goes out of business tomorrow? It's just one platform, after all. What happens to your earning ability then?

Maybe you'd scramble to make accounts on other freelance marketplaces. Problem is, it takes time to build up a reputation on new sites. So if you only use one platform, you're entirely at their mercy. They don't even have to go under— they might just change and become terrible to use.

If you rely on only Upwork or any single platform, you're placing your income at risk.

Instead, create a profile on at least three sites. You can certainly favor one or two of them, but at least give the others a shot occasionally.

Better yet, build your own personal writing website and post great content so you start to get organic traffic from Google. This way, you'll be calling the shots and not paying any platform fees. It will take time for Google to rank your content so your site shows up in search results, but eventually good content will be rewarded with site traffic. If you play your cards right and optimize your site for conversion, those site visitors could easily turn into leads and clients and potentially repeat clients.

Repeat clients are fantastic because they often mean more steady work and because you'll develop a feel for working together. In time you may find that a few really good repeat clients make up the majority of your income. At that point, you'll start to be less dependent on using freelancing sites to find daily work. It's all about doing everything you can to maintain your independence and consistent earning ability.

To maximize your chances of getting a job and keeping a constant flow of work, sign up for at least 2-3 different hiring platforms. You can use basically the same information on all the platforms, so it's not going to be too time consuming.

Part III - Freelance Business Basics

In this chapter, we'll get into nuts and bolts of how to actually set up and market your freelance business. A lot of this is going to be the same regardless of what business you're starting, but there are some things that are specific to freelancing in the cannabis space.

Should I Do it Solo, or Find a Team?

Let's say you find a cannabis copywriter, technical writer and web developer. You now have a team, meaning, you can handle any type of job thrown at you. If one member of the team can't handle a particular job, he or she turns it to the next person. This reduces incidences of lost income, since you'll be able to take on jobs that one of you alone couldn't handle. Plus, you'll have fresh eyes to look at your work before you submit, which is extremely valuable

Naturally, working together with others to create an agency will carry with it lots of potential risks. There's no surer stress-test for a group of people than starting a business together (ok maybe starting a marriage or a band is worse). If things go smoothly and you can get your egos in check and work together it can be amazing. You'll be able to create things that one of you wouldn't be able to do alone. But just know that your relationship with your co-founders will be tested at times. Proceed with caution on teaming up with partners, but do give it some consideration.

Developing a Professional Network

One of the most important things you can do to ensure the success of your business is to make sure to build up a good professional network. Professional networking is simply building professional relationships. It's about meeting and establishing mutually-beneficial connections with people who are in the same profession or industry as you. The goal is to build a group of people who you would happily do a favor for— and they would do the same for you. It's about reciprocity. You scratch my back I scratch yours.

What kinds of benefits are we talking about here? Well, for one, you're more likely to hear about any new job opportunities in your niche or even be recommended to the hirer by somebody in your network. Having a solid professional network will help you in your job searching and could open up doors to otherwise impossible-to-find career opportunities.

Start With Dormant Ties

When it comes to people, most of us have a tendency of meeting people and then falling out of touch. We rarely follow up on the connections we make. Let me ask, how many unused business cards or numbers do you have on your phone? Plenty, right? One method of starting to build your professional network is by following up with these "dormant ties". Dormant ties are people or friends you used to be close with but nowadays you don't catch up with. The thing to realize is, it is far easier to build a network with people you know or knew than it is with new people, why? They are not strangers. Maybe it'll take some courage, but reaching out to people from our past is a great way to jumpstart your network.

How do I start to build a network?

- Attend trade shows and industry-related physical gatherings.
- Attend online industry webinars and meetings.
- Ask people you already know to introduce you to people in the business.
- Email other freelancers whose work you like. Tell them how amazing they are!
- Interact with other industry brands and businesses on social media.
- Check out local meetups and networking events.

Contracts With Clients

Contracts are a huge pain, but they can protect you from huge headaches and potentially even lawsuits. The benefit of a contract between you and your client is simply to make sure expectations are clear and agreed upon by all parties.

They're designed to make things easier for everybody. Nobody can say, "well, you didn't say I had to do *that*" and the client can't say "I don't feel like paying you". It protects everybody involved.

In all honesty, contracts are probably not needed for simple Upwork writing jobs, as long as the expectations on the original job post are clear. Most of what you are doing is covered by the platforms user agreement. In case of disputes, Upwork can function as an arbitrator to some degree and help clear up disagreements between freelancers and clients. This should only be a last resort— not something to rely on all the time. For that reason, it's often a good idea that you have a real contract for higher-value jobs and jobs of greater complexity.

One important element you should always make sure to include in contracts with clients is a kill fee or cancellation fee. Basically, if things go south between you and the client and the job sours, this contract clause will save you from not getting all the money you have worked to earn.

If the project is terminated for whatever reason, (maybe the client goes bankrupt or cancels the project, etc.) the client is still required to pay you for the time you've already put into the project.

You could, for example, specify that the already paid deposit is non-refundable and will serve as the kill fee in case of contract termination. There will usually also be a provision so that you're compensated for any other expenses for the work already done.

The idea here is that you want to be able to get paid for any work you've done if something goes wrong. You may find that there are some clients that can just be too problematic and it can be easier to terminate the contract than to continue with the bad working relationship. Remember when I said you can fire clients? You can and you should fire clients if they really are causing you problems.

Terminating the contract will mean that the client doesn't have to pay you for any work you didn't do yet, but it also means that you're free to work on other work.

You can write a contract yourself if you have experience doing that, but even if you do it's probably best to find a good template contract to start from. Better yet, if you have the budget for it, it's a much safer idea to have a lawyer draw up a contract for you. Just another reason why having a good lawyer in your professional network is a powerful asset.

A Freelance Contract Should Always Include:

- Contact details from Freelancer and Client
- Project scope
- Deliverables
- Pricing and rates
- Payment schedule and options
- Milestones, deadlines and timeline
- Ownership / Copyright
- Legal terms
- Kill fee and cancellation terms
- Signatures
- Anything else that affects the freelancer-client relationship
- Any potential complication of this specific job

Accounting for Freelancers

When tax time comes around it's crucial that you keep excellent records of any business related expenses. You absolutely should have a separate business credit card and business bank account for this purpose. If you commingle your personal funds and business funds, it's going to be extremely tough to keep organized. If you're not organized it's easy to overlook perfectly legal business deductions when you go to file your taxes. Keep a close eye on every possible deduction so that you can avoid paying any more tax than you absolutely have to.

Although your accounting system can be as simple as a spreadsheet, my personal recommendation is to use something like Freshbooks or Quickbooks Online. This way, all you have to do is set it up with your credit card accounts and bank accounts and it can automatically track and organize your purchases and expenses. This can save you a ton of time, but remember that it's not 100% hands off. You'll still need to go in once in a while to check and make sure expenses go to the correct categories and so on. You'll also still need to keep physical receipts for anything that you paid cash for and enter those manually since they won't automatically show up like card purchases.

Accounting can get complicated so it's probably a good idea to find an accountant you trust and stick with them. If bookkeeping is something completely new for you, there are some awesome classes on business bookkeeping available on sites like Skillshare or Udemy. You can usually sign up for these platforms for a limited time free trial.

Popular Deductions for US-Based Freelancers

Here are some popular deductions for freelancers who file taxes in the United States. Remember, don't try to BS the IRS and always double-check with your CPA!

1. **Office Supplies** - Things like printer cartridges, paper, books, pencils, pens, and paper clips.

2. **Hardware and Software** - Any hardware or software you use to run the business can be deducted. If you use your personal laptop, smartphone, or tablet for work too, you may be able to deduct those and anything else you use for your business like cameras, accounting software, etc.
If you keep a written log that shows that you do use hardware and software for work too, you can claim the business percentage.

3. **Advertising** - Any ads, brochures, sponsored posts, business cards, or other promo stuff you buy to promote your business.

Fun tip— if you print your logo on your clothes you can deduct those clothes! Just embroider that awesome vest you want with your logo and it's deductible! The branding needs to be very clear in order to qualify for this deduction.

4. Health Insurance - If you had a net profit from self-employment for the year, you can usually deduct any medical, dental, or long term care insurance premiums that you've paid. The IRS states, "If you are self-employed, the IRS wants you to know about a tax deduction generally available to people who are self-employed.".

5. Insurance Premiums - These would be premiums for things like worker's compensation insurance, liability insurance, malpractice insurance, or fire, flood, storm, or theft insurance.

6. Travel Expenses - If you travel for business for things like trade shows, events, client meetings, or similar business related purposes, you may be able to deduct things like flights, car rentals, or hotel rooms. You can combine vacations with business, but you'll only be able to deduct the business portion.

7. Membership Dues - If you're a member of any organizations that assist with your freelance career and charges fees, those fees can be written off your taxes.

8. Research Materials - Say you just decided to write a book about pest removal practices for organic cannabis growers. If you bought books or any other research materials to help you write that book, those are deductible. Unfortunately, you can't write off weed itself since it's still federally illegal. Maybe someday soon you'll be able to buy some fresh buds, do a review of them for your blog, and write of the cost of the nugs.

9. **Phone and Internet Bills** - If you use your phones or internet for personal and business purposes, you can usually only deduct the business portion.

10. **Online Presence** - This could be considered advertising in a way, but any tools like MailChimp, HootSuite, or LinkedIn that you use to maintain your online presence can be deducted on your taxes. This also includes any website costs such as domain name registration and website hosting fees.

11. **Professional and Legal Services** - Any trips to the accountant or the lawyer should be deducted.

12. **Interest** - Credit card interest and any interest on business related loans can be deducted.

13. **Transaction Fees** - Any fees paid to sites like Paypal can be deducted.

14. **Retirement Plan Contributions** - If you pay into a retirement plan such as a SEP IRA, whatever you put in is deductible.

15. **Depreciation** - This is an annual allowance for wear and tear on items that are used over a set period of time. For example, your accountant might advise you to depreciate the cost of your new laptop over an estimated lifespan of that device rather than using the deduction for just one year. The IRS describes this as "an income tax deduction that allows a taxpayer to recover the cost or other basis of certain property. It is an annual allowance for the wear and tear, deterioration, or obsolescence of the property."

16. **Contract Labor** - If you hired any other independent contractors or freelancers on sites like Upwork, then those expenses can be deducted. For example, if you hired someone to design you a logo or make you a website or write a blog post you didn't have time for, those are write offs.

17. **Self Employment Tax** - If you're filing a Form 1040 Schedule C, then you can typically deduct half the cost of Social Security and Medicare taxes. After a while, you may eventually benefit from forming a LLC or an S-Corp, since this could lower the amount of self-employment taxes that you're responsible for. Check with a CPA.

18. **Educational and Professional Development Expenses** - Any education you spend money on to help with your business is tax deductible. This includes things like conferences, classes, mentors, coaches, etc.

19. **Car and Truck Expenses** - This is another one where you can only write off a percentage of business related vehicle use. If you rely on the vehicle for your business; you may be able to deduct payments, gas, and maintenance. Check with your accountant on this one since the terms are complex and it's a little tricky to keep track of usage.

20. **Unpaid Invoices** - Another tricky one, but you may have the ability to write off any unpaid invoices from the last year as bad debt. For you to deduct unpaid invoices, you would have to have claimed this as income first.

21. **Taxes and Licenses** - The IRS allows you to deduct federal unemployment tax, and State and local taxes. If you're in a specific field that requires you to have an occupational title then the cost of these licenses can be claimed.

22. **Maintenance and Repairs** - If you have something you use for your business and you need to have it repaired, the repair cost is deductible. Dropped your laptop? The repair is deductible.

23. **Meals** - The IRS has strict guidelines regarding the deduction of meals. If you take your client to a business meal at a restaurant,

then you can probably write that expense off. If you went on a weeklong vacation to Hawaii with the client, the IRS might not be happy.

24. Office Space - This is usually the biggest deduction that a freelancer will claim. You need to do most of your work from home for this to apply, but it doesn't matter if you own or rent that home. As of this writing, you can claim "$5 a square foot for up to 300 square feet." according to the IRS,

Outsourcing Writing to Get More Work Done

What happens if your marketing efforts start paying off and you find yourself getting more job offers than you can handle? It seems like a good problem to have and it can be, but only if you're prepared for it.

There may come a time when you have more client requests than you can reasonably do yourself. Better to consider and start planning for that now so you're ready when it happens.

One of the most beautiful things about running a freelance writing business is that *you don't have to do all the work.*

Taking some of the work off your plate by outsourcing some projects is beneficial in that you earn even when you are not working. Let's say you land a project worth $500. If you outsource the job, or find a person willing to do the job at half the amount. You get to keep the rest. That's an easy $200 or more (depending on platform fees) in your pocket.

Some freelancers get to a point where they stop doing most of the writing themselves. Instead, they get pretty good at getting work and delegating jobs to other freelancers. At that point it becomes more about people skills and managing responsibilities than about the actual writing.

For this to work, you need to get lots of different writers so you can find a few reliable ones. They can be the ones helping you to draft the writing and your task can be to review, revise, and send the finished product to the client.

Native english speaking freelance writers have a distinct advantage that English is their first tongue. For that reason, it is easier for a native to land high paying jobs than it is for someone to whom English is a second language.

This doesn't mean that non-natives can't deliver high quality writing on schedule.

You will find things like "Native English speakers only" or "US freelancers only".

in many jobs posted on Upwork and other freelance sites. Adding the phrase weeds out a huge chunk of writers. Why not take advantage of that? You could potentially be the middleman i.e. find good nonnative writers, programmers, or coders and work with them so you can earn more.

Agencies: Teaming Up With Other Freelancers

Instead of going it as a loner, another possibility is to team up with other freelancers that have complementary skill sets. Assume that you have an editor, web developer, writer, marketer, and graphic designer in-house. That means you are providing several different services a potential client might need all under one roof. This has the potential to earn you more money as well, because clients no longer have to hire more freelancers to fill in the gaps. Kind of like creating a one stop shop for everything cannabis related.

Finding A Team To Work With

One, you can look for people close to home or two, tap into the same freelance marketplaces that clients use. Upwork provides you this option in the form of 'Agency'. That is, the company allows you to partner with other freelancers from all over the planet.

When choosing freelancers to team up with, you'll want to choose freelancers that have skill sets that will help you best meet the needs of your target clients. For example, if you find many of your clients are new startups that need website copywriting and that they also need new websites, you might consider bringing a web designer/developer onboard. The idea is to figure out what clients need most so you and your team can consider adding those services.

Do your homework and thoroughly vet any freelancers that you're thinking about working together with on any project. If they fail to deliver, it's going to make you look terrible and probably get your agency a negative review from that client.

Teaming up and forming agencies like this isn't for everybody, but if it's something that you find appealing, here are a few specialties that you might consider partnering with:

1. Other freelance cannabis writers and copywriters
2. Copy editors and proofreaders
3. Web developers or programmers
4. Freelancer photographers
5. Search engine optimization expert's (SEO)
6. Graphic designers
7. Mobile app developers
8. Admin support or assistant
9. Ad specialists
10. Translation
11. Web research

Communicating With A Team of Freelancers

To manage a group of freelancers you'll first need to get organized, which will require good communication. Figure out how you are going to communicate with your team members in a way that best suits your team. Upwork does have a built in messaging system and it's actually not that bad for the most part. Keeping your conversations there is one way to keep everyone on the same page and accountable. Slack is another common choice for team communication and it has free plans available.

Part IV: Branding & Marketing

Once you've got the business started and you're working on getting more clients, the next question becomes, how do I get noticed? In this section we'll briefly go over some different methods you can use to fine-tune your brand and market it..

Getting Yourself Noticed: Branding

On to branding. We touched on branding briefly earlier when we talked about what to name your business. But branding has to do with more than just what you call your business, it's about creating a personality for your business. It encompasses nearly every aspect of your business from your logo to the sort of voice you use to speak to your customers to the feel of the fonts on your website. Here are four important tactics to building your brand.

1. Showcase Your Personality

The first thing you have to do is showcase your personality. Take for instance the photo of you that you put on your about page. Instead of posting some boring straight business headshot, try to post a photo of you that tells more of a story about who you are. Maybe it's as simple as having your dog in the photo with you. Instantly it says, you're fun (because you didn't use a bland photo) and you love dogs. Or at least one dog. This, in your audience's eyes makes you more of a real person. You're relatable. That's the power of showing a little of your personal style.

2. Craft Your Online Presence To Fill Your Client's Needs

Whether you decide to create your own website or simply a profile on a freelance site like Upwork, it's important to make yourself look like the perfect candidate for the job. The first step towards making that impression on clients is to simply pay attention to what they want. The better you know what they want, the easier you can try to become their ideal candidate. Here we're talking about tweaking your online profiles to emphasize the skills you have that match your ideal client's requirements.

3. Keep an Updated Portfolio

Most clients will only read the first few pieces in your portfolio, but that doesn't mean that you should stop updating it. What you include in your portfolio serves as evidence that you can write. It should go without saying, but everything you put up, should be written to your best ability and thoroughly proofread.

4. Define Yourself With Your Writing Style

Originality is a tough nut to crack, especially, in the world of freelancing. Working to develop your own unique writing style is certainly something worth pursuing. To some extent, it's very natural for your early writing in any new genre to take on the style of other writers you like. It's the same with any art and it's not something to worry about. In time, your original style will take shape on it's own. Almost without you being aware of it at all.

5. Personalize Your Marketing Messages

Personalizing the message of your marketing content goes beyond merely adding first names to your email greeting. It requires digging into your prospect's mind and discovering what they fear, wish, and want. You need to convey to your consumers that you understand their pain points and want to help.

6. Segment Your Marketing Messages

Segmentation, refers to separating audience members into groups based on their actions; things like first-time purchases, abandoned carts, repeat purchases, page views, etc. Data-driven segmentation like this allows you to tailor your marketing messages to specific customers or leads that have taken specific actions— usually on your website. For example, by segmenting your audience like this, you can make sure that the marketing email you send to a person who signed up for your email list is different than one you send to former clients. Segmenting marketing messages based on what point in the customer journey people are at will help you craft your messages more precisely.

7. Keep Your Marketing Current

Timeliness also proves to be a critical part of any successful marketing strategy, as readers don't want to be bombarded with dated content that has become irrelevant. Make sure you are constantly monitoring old content like blog posts and any advertisements to see if they need to be refreshed and updated.

Marketing Options To Consider

It's important that you find a marketing approach that works for you. The options here are unlimited, but some popular methods include:

- Starting a website to share your writing and talk openly about your business.
- Do some pro-bono work for a company you really believe in.
- Answer questions on sites like Quora pertaining to your specialty.
- Engage social media and show brand personality.
- Choose a cause and run with it: research shows 50% of millennials in the US are more willing to buy from a business that supports a cause they believe in.
- Soliciting public reviews from previous clients.
- Collaborating with other businesses in the industry.
- Build a social media presence.
- Write a book related to your niche.
- Start a podcast.
- Create an educational YouTube channel
- Teach a copywriting course on sites like Skillshare, Udemy, etc.
- Guest post on industry blogs and magazines

- Offer free content online: if you have a website or blog, write helpful weed articles and posts.
- Join groups: join both local and online cannabis writer's groups on sites like Facebook (network). You should also take advantage of LinkedIn's pro-finder feature which sends clients to your profile based on services you offer for a small fee.
- Create a specialized profile on freelance sites: tailor your unique skills to your audience on your chosen site.

Creating a Blog to Showcase Your Writing

A fantastic way to grow your skills and market yourself is by starting an informational site that has to do with cannabis in some way. Maybe there's a specific cannabis niche that you feel drawn to personally or maybe there's just a topic you feel like learning more about. For example, maybe you really love sharing the healing power of cooking with weed. You could start a website focused on providing recipes and educational resources related to cannabis cooking.

Let's say that you go for it. You start a cannabis cuisine site and consistently publish new articles to it. Over time, people start to find your content and your site becomes very popular. Not only that, but you're able to use all this writing as valuable portfolio material to show to paying clients.

You keep posting to your site and your posts get better and better and eventually, your site is so popular you have new monetization opportunities such as ad revenue, sponsored posts, endorsements, and all sorts of influencer collaborations. Your authority in the marijuana niche is now there for everybody to see

Starting a blog may seem intimidating at first, but it's something you can learn pretty fast if you're motivated. If you're savvy with websites you can have a Wordpress website up in less than a day. It doesn't need to look beautiful at first, since at first there won't be a whole lot of people reading it.

If this all sounds way beyond your skills at the moment, you can also hire someone on Upwork to make you a site. It will cost you upfront, but it's a valuable (and tax deductible) investment in your business.

Produce Content That People Value

The easiest and most effective way of connecting with any audience is by providing valuable original content. Blogging is one of the most effective ways of doing that.

See the thing is, even if you spend thousands of dollars on advertising, it doesn't guarantee returning customers. What guarantees returning customers is value.

What are they getting from you that they can't get from somewhere else? In other words, what's in it for them?

Give Your Best Stuff Away For Free

Your writing can be used to educate others as well as to bolster your professional authority. Don't be afraid to give away your work for free in this way. Instead of keeping all that knowledge locked up in your noodle, share it!

Share Your Posts With As Many People as Possible

As long as your site is properly made and optimized for search, Google will eventually find your content and index it. But that doesn't mean you shouldn't be self-promoting it as well. You want to do everything you can to get exposure and traffic to your writing.

Publicizing your site content could easily be a book in itself, but to reach as many heads as possible, you need to find people who are passionate about the niche you write for. If you make a site having to do with cannabis legal issues, you'll likely want to find out where other people with that interest spend time online. That way you can tactfully share your posts to popular sites they frequent. You can share details of your posts on sites like Digg, Reddit, Facebook, Twitter, relevant forums, YouTube, LinkedIn, or any other site that your market favors.

Search Intent Explained

Search intent refers to the user's end goal when typing a query into a search engine.

In general, you should always be writing with search intent in mind. By this I mean that you should always be visualizing the sort of reader you're looking to grab with your writing. What's that person searching for? And more importantly, how can you write something that's just what they're looking for?

Letting Data Inform Your Blogs Content Plan

1. Plan your blog content with proper keyword research.
2. Find and use semantic keywords.
3. Write strong headlines or effective blog post titles.
4. Make internal linking a habit.
5. Add and optimize videos and images to your blog posts.
6. Add meta-descriptions to your blog posts.
7. Make your articles user friendly and easy to read.
8. Organize your content using categories and tags.

Aim for Google's Featured Snippet Spot

Position zero, instant answers, it goes by different names but you know what I'm talking about, right? When you key in a query on google, you may have noticed that google pulls content that's already ranking and uses it to answer questions.

For example, if I type in how to make cannabutter, I get a recipe right there in the Google search results. No need to even click through to visit the site it's from! The benefit of this is that most people will still click through to your site and read more.

It's not easy to get your content featured in this way but there are some things you can do to increase your chances. To help your odds of getting the featured snippet spot, try these techniques:

- Answer popular questions directly.
- Give the answer near the beginning of the post **in bold.**

- Write how-to-guides and include summaries in list posts.
- Provide immediate, clear and concise answers.

Getting the Most Mileage From Your Content

Once you get in the habit of blogging, make sure you do not forget the content you've already published! Updating old content is a proven strategy that will keep your site looking fresh and relevant. Google has a freshness ranking factor on its search engine; most sites eventually see content decay and fall out of favor.

There are old articles that have ranked well and attracted generous amounts of backlinks in the past, but now they show a significant reduction in search traffic for that particular article. After a series of testing, it was discovered that making simple updates and tweaks to an existing article made its ranking improve significantly.

Importantly, changing the date— to represent the newest revision—made site content appear fresh so that search engines don't rank them to the back pages. It's no secret that Google prefers fresh content, but you might not have anticipated the solution to be so easy and effective.

Also, just because you posted content on one channel doesn't mean you shouldn't find a way to use it on other channels to promote your brand.

No, you probably shouldn't just repost exactly the same thing you post on Facebook to instagram and your website. However you can *and should* adapt your content to use in as many places as possible. It's smart business to get as much bang for your buck as possible out of everything you create.

For example, you could turn blog content into podcasts or videos. The majority of the background research and writing has already been done, so you'll just need to slightly adapt the content for its new role.

Cannabis Niche Sites & Affiliate Marketing

Creating a cannabis affiliate marketing "niche" site could be a fantastic way to add some passive income to your freelance writing game.

By definition, affiliate marketing is an arrangement where an online retailer pays you a commission for sales generated from a referral. When a person buys something you referred to on your site, you get paid.

Referrals are typically tracked either via a unique tracking link, or by using a unique promo code. For example, if you are writing a blog with lots of educational articles about CBD supplements for dogs, it would be totally reasonable to include affiliate links to CBD oils that you recommend. Your readers would get valuable information and product recommendations for free so it's a win win for them.

To make use of affiliate marketing as a writer, you could create a new site for a niche within the cannabis space. You could do reviews of rolling papers for example and teach joint rolling. This is a great way to practice your writing, build your portfolio, and possibly earn some passive income over time.

If you have a blog on your personal freelancing site where you talk about writing, you can also put affiliate links on there for any products you make use of and want to share. So if you happen to, for example, read a *fantastic* book on becoming a freelance cannabis writer, you can talk about it on your writing blog and include an affiliate URL to Amazon where your readers can buy it and make you extra cash. That book writer will love you for doing that too, most likely.

A deep dive into affiliate marketing is beyond the scope of this book, but it's definitely something worth looking into and learning more about. Many of your clients are likely to be affiliate marketers in some way themselves and will value your knowledge of the techniques. Towards the end of this book there is a section on devising a content marketing strategy, and that advice will be very helpful for creating an affiliate site content plan if you go down that route.

Show Your Expertise By Guest Posting

In the right hands, guest blog posts can be used to get high-quality backlinks to your website, and you can use them to gain exposure for your brand. What is a guest post? Guest posting is simply writing articles on another blog in the same niche. Usually you won't be talking directly about your product or business, but instead you'll be writing informative content that would appeal to the same sort of reader. The site that you write a guest post for gets free content, and you get your name and usually a link to your site. But first you'll need to get your work in front of website editors.

Editors are busy people. Every day, depending on the site's popularity, editors may have to go through dozens if not hundreds of guest post pitches. To stand out from the competition, your articles need to be expertly crafted to appeal to the site's readership.

The editors of makealiving.com recently published an article titled "9 Top Online Editors Vent About Writers" where they gathered some common grievances that editors have about guest post submissions.

The editors all agreed that:

- Doing your research is crucial.
- Image content, size, and quality matters.
- Header tag use is crucial.
- Post ideas need to be on-topic and appropriate.
- Pitch emails need to be well written.
- Nobody likes mass emails— avoid BCC.
- Grammar and spelling matters.
- Follow the guidelines set by the editor.

Content marketing for Cannabis & CBD Brands

The brands that make up the cannabis industry, in general, are fighting for limited online space.

They're fighting for *your* eyes on *their* content and what they're selling.

This war is largely fought via SEO, and by providing high quality, useful content. Why?

Because providing valuable content to your target audience for free is an excellent way to get those precious eyes on your brand.

And that's all content marketing is, really; anything you create and share that your customers find value in.

As a freelancer you'll need to take care to market yourself every chance you can get, and content marketing is a great way to get your site organic traffic passively over time. The great thing is they do this for free after they're written as opposed to ads that stop working the second you stop paying for them) .

However you choose to personally market yourself via your content, it's in your best interest to know the basics of content marketing so you can write persuasive copy for your clients.

With the limitations on cannabis advertising and marketing still very real, content marketing is a powerful technique to master. Let's learn how to grow your cannabis marketing strategy with content marketing.

It's what we do every day here at Leaf Writers, and if it didn't work we wouldn't do it. Because nobody would keep paying us.

So let's take a deep dive into creating an effective content strategy for your cannabis brand.

What is Cannabis Content Marketing?

Content marketing simply entails offering relevant (and free) information to your niche audience.

Sounds simple. Is Simple. But also simple to get wrong.

Most businesses in the cannabis space know what content marketing is and have some sort of content plan in place. Content marketing is trending hard and people know about it, but many companies aren't doing it effectively.

It's common to see cannabis and CBD brands running mismanaged, ineffective strategies that aren't likely to move the needle on their bottom line.

Or they have no plan at all. Don't be them.

Tools of Content Marketing

As we mentioned, it's all about sharing content (information) in some form or another. And **there are a ton of different ways to share content**. Mostly commonly though, you'll be sharing your content through one or more of these channels:

- Email
- Blog Posts
- Podcasts
- Social media posts
- Infographics
- Webinars

Keep in mind that there are many, many other content marketing channels as well. Some of these channels are very niche-focused and could be a fantastic way to reach your consumer in a way they prefer. Bottom line, so it's a great idea to check out all options beyond the big ones so you see which is most appropriate for your exact market.

No matter the channel, your content will educate your audience or otherwise give them something they value. Usually related to the market you're in.

Your content is not meant to talk only about your products or services or brand exclusively. It's meant to give your audience something they're looking for— for free.

That way you can earn their loyalty and, hopefully, they'll remember you and keep coming back.

It all comes down to making your specific audience feel good and happy about your brand, often by solving a particular problem. And you do this by simply providing relevant, informative, entertaining content on a regular basis.

What Can Cannabis Content Marketing Do?

Get Your Brand Seen Without Paid Ads

Running paid ads can be extremely problematic right now for cannabis and CBD brands. Federal prohibition, rapidly changing state laws, and the prohibitive policies of advertising platforms generally make it impossible to run ads on the major platforms.

Search engines like Google, Bing, and Yahoo follow stringent policies not to publish advertisements encouraging the use of cannabis in any form.

But there's absolutely nothing prohibiting cannabis brands from pumping out awesome SEO content that ranks organically in search engines. And that's precisely what's going to allow people to find you without typical ads

You have full leeway in developing a website for the purpose of advertising your marijuana brand, and employing legitimate SEO approaches for securing a good rank on Google.

That right there makes content marketing hugely powerful and worth the investment but wait, there's more!

Establish Authority in Your Niche

If you regularly create valuable content for your audience and share it correctly, there's a good shot that your audience will appreciate it and share it.

Maybe they'll share it on facebook, reddit, instagram, or some other social site. Maybe they'll show they appreciate it by linking to it on their website. Either way, you win.

You'll win because it's this sharing that signals to Google that your content (and your website) deserves to be found.

When you post lots of useful well written content on a topic, Google will eventually learn this and start placing your site higher up in people's search results.

Not overnight, but it'll happen.

Your blog article or instagram post might initially only be seen/read by a small number of people, but if it's shared socially or linked to from another site it can easily blow up.

The more your content gets passed around, the more your brand starts to look like authority on the topic - both in the eyes of both your customers and to Google. And Google richly rewards those who please its algorithmic eyes.

Make Your Customers Your Ambassadors

The beauty is that if all goes as planned, your potential customers will be not only discovering you through your content but also by passing your sweet sweet cannabis content around.

It's almost as if they're doing your marketing legwork for you.

They'll be indirectly helping you market your brand and position it as a trustworthy authority— the kind they might someday want to do business with.

And of course, your customers are always your most reliable and steadfast brand ambassadors.

Boosted loyalty and retention

You will be able to connect with your audience more effectively if you offer them customized content. Several market research surveys and studies indicate that customers prefer reading content about brands they like rather than clicking on ads.

Keeps Your Brand On Their Mind

You might not write about your own products and services directly, but your content will still educate your readers on your brand and its overall style.

Ever heard of the rule of seven?

"The rule of seven simply says that the prospective buyer should hear or see the marketing message at least seven times before they buy it from you."

In other words, the chance of a prospective buyer turning into a sale isn't super likely the first time they see or hear about you. It does however greatly increase each time they're exposed to some content from your brand.

Content marketing should help in promotion and endorsement by getting customers mentally familiar with your company, even if they're not yet in a position to be a paying customer.

Reach Customers The Way They Want to be Reached

Most people don't love ads. They don't love blatant advertising in general. Most would prefer to connect with your brand through some useful content than through invasive advertisements. They'd rather learn about you at a time and on a channel they decide.

In this way, you can think of ads a shotgun approach whereas your content is more akin to a sniper rifle. Sure, ads target keywords so it's not exactly a great analogy, but you're picking up what I'm putting down right?

By offering people relevant info in a way they like it, you can show that your brand *gets* their audience. And it's really important that your brand gets your audience. They'll know if you're a fake.

Helps You Compete With Larger Companies

You can take on big businesses that spend millions for promoting their product or service by making the most of content marketing.

You might not have the same content budget as the big players, but don't let that stop you. The best content isn't necessarily the most expensive content - the best content is what resonates best with *your target market.*

Helps Generate Brand Awareness

The best thing about content marketing is that it is not humdrum and repetitive like traditional promotional channels. At the same time, content marketing is more cost-effective than most other types of traditional or digital marketing mediums. Content marketing can help create awareness about your brand in an understated manner and without being disruptive.

Must-haves for Effective Cannabis Content Marketing

Since your brand's content is a big part of how your clients interact with your brand, it absolutely needs to be carefully considered. Good content marketing should:

Include Content That's Relatable and Easily Understood

The content should be created and presented in a way that your particular audience can understand easily and personally relate to. It also needs to hold their attention. This doesn't mean dumbing down your content, but just making it appropriate for the nature of your product.

For example, you'll likely want to use a lot more medical terminology for dispensary copywriting than you might for a line of rolling papers. Additionally, the information the establishment shares via the content should be engaging enough to hold the audience's attention.

Should Be Informative

Don't just tell your customers you know your stuff - show them by teaching them things they don't already know (but want to know).

The content might inform customers about the various active compounds and ingredients abounding in cannabis or the effects of a particular strain. The actual topic will depend on your niche in the cannabis industry. The long and short of it all is that the informative content (marketing) is something your audience will value and appreciate you for providing.

Give Your Audience What It Wants

Your blog posts, social media posts, and any other content you put out should offer exactly what your audience prefers rather than providing info in some boring generic way. You can bet your audience will keep revisiting your site if you can consistently offer them what they're looking for. When you're first getting started, it will be harder to gauge exactly what kind of content will resonate best with your audience. One way to approach this is to try out several styles of content. Trying a few different things at ones will let you quickly see what sorts of content to make more of and what isn't working. Signing up for a Google Analytics account will allow you to dive deep into what efforts are performing best. In this way, you'll be letting hard data guide your future content marketing.

Stay Neutral & Don't Excessively Promote Your Products

Though your chief goal is to use your content to entice the audience into trusting and buying from your brand, you still need to be somewhat subtle about the whole thing.

Cannabis buyers are savvy and can smell sales jargon a mile away. They're no fools, they know you're posting your content to get them to buy.

The great thing is that even though your niche segment is acutely aware of the underlying motive behind your content strategy, it doesn't stop it from being effective.

9 Examples of Great Cannabis Content Marketing

The axiom 'A good wine needs no bush' was perfectly applicable to the cannabis industry. Cannabis businesses and brands flourished and thrived for decades without having to bank on branding and promotion.

But those days are quickly dawning and nowadays great content is the way your cannabis brand will set itself apart.

In this section, we review 9 top cannabis brands and how they are taking optimum advantage of content marketing for promoting their business.

Leafly

Launch a search on your web browser for 'cannabis' or for any other keyword linked with the drug, and chances are that you'll always find Leafly's URL on the first search results page. Leafy is one of the most popular websites dedicated to cannabis and everything associated with the drug.

The website claims to be the largest online dispensary of medical marijuana strains and customers can use Leafly to study the most trending strains that have been ranked based on customer reviews. Leafly also posts blog content relating to cannabis regularly.

https://www.leafly.com/

Kiva Confections

Founders Kristi Palmer and Scott Palmer saw that the cannabis edibles (when the legal cannabis market in the state was still evolving) were flavorless, had inconsistent potency, and poorly packaged. The couple had a brainstorm after visiting a neighborhood chocolatier: blend cannabis with chocolate.

And that is how Kiva Confections came into being. Kiva handcrafts every one of its Terra Bites and Kiva Bars using coldwater hashish, ensuring chemical-free and pure THC concentrates. Kiva has teamed up with veteran cultivators and chocolatiers that supply the best quality of weed and cocoa.

https://kivaconfections.com/news/kiva-chocolate-cold-water-hash

Wana Edibles

Medical marijuana users and weed buffs will instantly take to Wana Edibles' advertising slogan' Wana enhance your life'? The landing page of Wana Edibles' website makes it clear that the company's chief objective is to promote the responsible use of the drug to enhance their quality of life.

Wana Edibles claims that the business promoters have made a lot of effort towards making every offering of top quality. The company deals exclusively with affordable edibles that can be used by recreational as well as medical cannabis users.

Rather than having a more standard blog with updates about the brand, Wana instead features a "learn" section on its website that focuses on educating its audience about the science and terminology of cannabis. The articles are all related to the sorts of products they sell, however it's important to notice that the articles are more general and not specific to their exact products.

https://wanabrands.com/

Marley Natural

Marley Natural promotes just four branded herbal products that you'd instinctively brand as run-of-the-mill products. However, the four products are regarded and celebrated as full-fledged lifestyle brands. The product line essentially comprises premium smoking accessories chiseled from black walnut wood and hemp seed body care products.

The brand name together with the mascot (the lion logo) resonates seamlessly with the legendary Jamaican singer-songwriter Bob Marley, also infamous for his weakness towards cannabis. Bob Marley courted controversy by openly advocating the legalization of marijuana. Marijuana enthusiasts will warm up to the fact that the site supports Marley's efforts for legalizing the use of cannabis.

At the same time, stoners will fall in love with the striking brand logo as well as the eye-catching packaging.

https://www.marleynaturalshop.com/

Willie's Reserve

A musician and instrumentalist famed for his weakness of cannabis launched the Willie's Reserve. The entire product line, including but not limited to a high five-pack, ready roll, and flower box, embody Willie's fascination for and infatuation with marijuana.

The brand image underscores Willie's notoriousness as an outlaw and his firmly rooted convictions about freedom and free will. Rival, an agency based in Santa Monica, CA, joined hands with Willie to help him launch his standalone cannabis line of products.

Though Willie is no more, he continues to live in Willie's Reserve- a premium marijuana range that has blazed a trail. Willie's fans, friends, and fellow musicians will corroborate that the singer along with his band, hopped from one town to another largely to hang out with stoners and weed enthusiasts.

www.williesreserve.com has a separate page devoted to blog posts. Cannabis enthusiasts will love to navigate on the site that has a minimalist yet appealing layout.

Lord Jones

Lord Jones is an extremely professional manufacturer of self-care CBD products and tinctures. If you use any of the products of

Lord Jones, you'll feel that you're in seventh heaven. That is how the 90,000 Instagram followers of the business feel.

And this following has almost doubled since 2018! Cannabis businesses will surely warm up to how the brand promotes itself via social media canvassing. Cannabis firms should take a look at the user-generated posts and take ideas from the same for building a relationship with their customers.

https://lordjones.com/

BEBOE

Enthusiasts of BEBOE (and its products, of course) admiringly regard the company as the 'Hermes of Marijuana.' You'll love the way how BEBOE infuses charm into the medical and THC cannabis culture.

https://www.beboe.com/

Take note of the brand's application of hashtags, otherworldly photography, and brief yet engaging taglines. The message that the brand conveys is something worth admiring. The brand has taken CBD to a new high.

NAAWK

NAAWK is perhaps the best instance of how to do content marketing right, Instagram content marketing to be precise. NAAWK also has a clear-cut niche audience-extreme sports enthusiasts and athletes who take CBD for recovering and rejuvenating after a grueling competitive or training session.

Cannabis firms and establishments can take inspiration from NAAWK's tenacity: it keeps on posting blogs on its Instagram profile with mechanical regularity. The business also makes the most of Instagram Highlights for putting the accents on its posts, news events, and stories.

https://naawk.com/

Charlotte's Web Hemp CBD

Charlotte's Web, the brainchild of Stanley Brothers from Colorado, is proving to be a veritable mover & shaker in the hemp/CBD market. Though the website is dedicated to pushing

CBD oil and hemp-based products, it keeps on posting informative blogs and posts on social media that are indeed edifying.

Most of the blog posts instruct parents and guardians about the beneficial effects of hemp CBD. You'll be pleasantly surprised to learn that not only adults use their topical, capsules, and hemp oils, but even kids use them, thanks to the brand's accessibility.

https://www.icharlotte.com/

Getting Started with a Cannabis Content Marketing Strategy

Without further adieu let's dig into the nitty gritty of adding a content marketing plan to your cannabis marketing strategy.

If you have an established site, you should first perform a content audit to get a better understanding of what content you've got and what's performing best.

Google Analytics is perfect for this task. You can easily see content that gets the most action and use Key Performance Indicators (KPIs) through the lifespan of your content.

You're looking for what's resonating with your audience so you can start applying what you learn to the new content you'll create. Keeping notes for improving your content is really helpful at this stage.

Besides just checking out your own content, it's important to also see what your competitors are up to with their content. That way you can see what's working for them and decide whether you should create something similar. After all, if it's working for them it should also work for you. **Under no circumstances should you copy your competitors content**— everything you create should be totally your own style and *hopefully* better than what the other guys are putting out.

At this stage it's also important to decide who's actually going to be doing the content creation. Who's the writer? Are you going to try and bootstrap and do everything yourself? Have your in-house team handle it? Outsource it to a freelancer or content agency (like us!).

Bottom line, you need to know what your content production process is going to look like.

Find Your Niche Segment

Without customers, you've got no business. Know your customers well.

Just like any other product or service-oriented business, your consumers are the lifeblood of your cannabis brand. Do a half-assed job defining your ideal buyer persona, and it's going to be difficult to craft content for your audience.

So, regardless of whether you're aggressively marketing THC tinctures, CBD oils, hemp edibles, or whatever it is, you'll need to identify your niche— and your target consumer first. This may sound scary, but really all it comes down to is getting to know your market and what motivates them.

You need to listen to what consumers are looking for so that your brand can create content that fills the gaps. You want to dig into pain points that you can provide solutions for.

Let your data inform the needs and goals of your content strategy.

Selecting Your Content Marketing Channels

Google will not allow you to post advertisements and classifieds that encourage the use of cannabis and ditto with the majority of social media platforms, including Facebook, Twitter, Instagram, and LinkedIn. However, these obstacles should not deter you from exploiting the digital domain for promoting your cannabis brand or brands.

Cannabis companies can also gain a lot of wisdom by following industry-related social media profiles. Firms can also attend social gatherings organized by the cannabis industry for forging strategic partnerships and also for sourcing prospective clients.

Instagram

Instagram followers are gung-ho about the social media site's innovative and state-of-the-art in-app shopping feature that is opening up new vistas. The social media platform's brand new shopping feature looks almost like an e-commerce mall. The site proudly declares that "the mall of the feature is not a sprawling metropolis of stores, punctuated by the occasional soft pretzel stand and a megaplex movie theater but a platform on your phone."

The in-app shop, aka digital mall, is akin to a large shopping complex, housing innumerable customized stores. The shopping app will carry your accounts and posts and present the storefront to your audience's news feed.

The platform's 'Explore' functionality collects, selects, and presents products posted based on the consumer's (or user's) needs and preferences. So, all you need to do is to create and update a blog and the same will be directed straightaway to your prospects' news feeds.

Cannabis content marketing guidelines for Instagram

- Social customer service: Social customer service helps in boosting brand loyalty as much as constructive customer experience does
- Organic: Focusing on organic search (like posting blogs regularly) helps in brand promotion as you are unable to exploit paid advertisements
- Create a responsive plan for dealing with customer problems: Don't wait until a problem occurs to figure out what to do. Have a responsive interaction strategy for dealing with probable problems your customers are likely to face. You can do what's called a "pre-mortem" to anticipate possible things that could go wrong.
- Make use of user-generated content: Highlight positive feedback and reviews of customers through recognized hashtags and announce awards and promotional offers
- Upload stories, videos, podcasts, and cannabis events

Facebook

You can create your business page on Facebook with a shopping template that enables you to connect your site to this social media platform. This feature lets your customers buy your product or subscribe to your service.

You can show your products by categories of price or usage as well as upload ads on your videos and posts. You can advertise your product or service using organic search, Facebook messenger/chatbot, videos, and publicize unique offers on Mobile Monkey for free

Twitter

You can make the most of Twitter's UX (user experience platform) for promoting your posts, news events, and trending topics. At the same time, you can make use of organic search, hashtags, and media forums and hubs for marketing your brand.

LinkedIn

Make the most of the following tips for publicizing your cannabis business on LinkedIn:-

- **Visuals:** Make optimum use of webcasts, podcasts, and thumb stoppers for attracting and arresting the attention of your consumers
- **Organic Search:** Create a receptive LinkedIn profile that will come in handy for uploading news, events, and occasions relating to the cannabis industry. Ensure to curate whatever you upload to keep your audience hooked regularly

Pinterest

This social network site also doubles up as a search engine and shopping network. So you can exploit this social media platform for creating brand awareness and improving sales. No, you cannot make use of paid promotions but always make the most of Pinnable graphics and user-generated content and posts for boosting traffic.

An excellent way to increase the traffic to your posts is to create pinterest-optimized images that are vertical and contain large text over a photo explaining what the article is about. Vertical photos are much more likely to be re-pinned, and hopefully clicked on by people interested in the topic.

Websites & Blogs

Google Ads still does not allow you to run ad campaigns revolving around cannabis but there's nothing to stop you from writing your blog and getting your content to rank organically. The great part is it can be totally free if you can do it all yourself. Or you can scale it to any size business. Works for all shapes and sizes.

Blogs are a particularly good content option for brands with a lot of heavy writing to share. Explaining the scientific process for extracting your new oil concentrate probably isn't going to go over well on photo-centric Instagram but it's perfect for a long form blog post. Create a fast-loading SEO friendly website and blog consistently so that Google can start ranking your pages and sending organic traffic your way.

Email

Remember right in the beginning of this book how I said to go to my site and site up for a free ebook? Getting a customer to subscribe to your newsletter is super valuable because it will allow you to keep your customers updated with new things you're working on and it will enable you to send them offers of things you think they'll enjoy and find value in. Email marketing is a hugely valuable tool to market yourself.

An engaged email subscriber list is worth its weight in gold, yet you'd be surprised how many brands overlook starting an email list until it's too late. You *absolutely* need to keep close track of your customers and email newsletters are a fantastic way to do that. They allow you to keep touch with your most devoted fans and tell them about new content. Make sure to create quality newsletters that don't focus on selling, but instead establish thought-leadership and brand awareness.

A content marketing plan is simply a schedule you keep of your publishing efforts. It's typically a spreadsheet or calendar, but there are also many online platforms to handle the same function. . Also, it's the step following your content strategy session.

Create a Content Schedule and Stick To It

It isn't all wine and roses. Content marketing requires a lot of work, patience, consistency and persistence. Not exactly everybody's favorite things.

The best content marketing strategy ever will do nothing for you if you aren't consistent with it. Being consistent with your plan is arguably the most important thing there is in content marketing.

Make a point of creating a set number of posts each week for each of the channels you're creating content for. Only with set goals can you consistently put out the content you'll need to grow your brand. And as ol' Tommy Edison would say, *"Opportunity is missed by most people because it is dressed in overalls and looks like work."*.

If you're willing to put in the work that your competitors are too lazy or preoccupied to do, you'll win over their customers in the long run— even if they've got more marketing dollars than you.

Craft Amazing Content

Once you've got a good idea of your niche, your ideal brand persona, and the marketing channels you plan to target, you can start to craft some awesome content that will appeal to that audience.

Don't write content just for the sake of it, but think critically about what your audience really needs right now. Your content should make it crystal clear that you *get* your audience and you're happy to provide them something they can benefit from.

Creating the content is of course going to be a very different process depending on which marketing channel(s) you decide to target. What works on Pinterest will not work on Facebook.

On the other hand, you can and should repurpose your content for use on other channels. As an example, you could do a podcast and then have the podcast transcribed and used as part of a blog post. You could also reuse your instagram photos as blog post images and so on. Get the most bang you can out of your content bucks.

Staying Consistent & Patient

There will certainly be days where it's tough to come up with creative ideas for your content— it happens to us all. But getting on a schedule where you post regular content will make the process so much easier

In the beginning it's going to be hard to get started and your content likely won't be very good (if you have no experience). But just show up and try to create anything. Start small. Don't try to create an amazing 5000 word whitepaper for a dispensary, start by posting daily 500 word posts to your blog.

There's a good chance you'll surprise yourself and it will come out way better than you expected. And gradually, that kind of consistency will get your writing canna-business some much deserved popularity.

Part V: Tips on The Craft

It's unrealistic to imagine ever being really good at anything until you've been at it for a while and dedicated yourself to improving. It's no different with writing. This chapter will focus on some tips for improving your craft as a writer as well as offering guidance on how to focus better, work more productively, and grow as a writer.

In the words of Aristotle. *"it is frequent repetition that produces a natural tendency"*. Keep your expectations realistic. Understand that no matter what you're trying to get good at, you're not going to master it without seriousness of purpose and practice. Lots of practice.

That means you do the same thing over and over until you develop self-assurance and skills that are worth paying for. There is no other way.

Writing never hurt anyone. So there! Start writing. Even if it's bad writing at first. And it likely will be. But suck it up and endure because the more you write the better you get at it. And it feels really good to get really good at something.

Putting Yourself in a Growth Mindset

Before you quit your day job and become a full-time cannabis writer. It is important to develop a writer's mindset. See the thing is. Writing Monday to Sunday is not an easy thing to do.

Your eyes will hurt, your back will hunch, your fingers will go numb and sometimes your brain will practically shut itself off. I am talking about the days where you feel totally burned out and unable to get the right words to come out.

A few key ways to practice a writer's mindset are:

- Continuously learn new skills and be willing to try new things.
- Play with ideas and Write with a purpose.
- Don't fear failure or embarrassment.
- Have the desire to improve your craft.

Rejection is Not A Rejection of You

See the thing is, a major difference between a seasoned professional and an amateur is that the professional handles criticism in the right way. They've learned to do this over time. Early on in your career it can be easier said than done to handle anybody badmouthing the precious literary baby you've labored over. When you've worked hard on something and you've got other deadlines to hit, then things can feel very personal. After a while though, your skin will thicken up and you'll be fine. If you keep at it. Which you will. To a professional, every day is a learning experience. A chance to improve your game.

There is no way around it. When it happens, rejection hurts. Sometimes a lot. But don't see rejection as the end of your road, instead use every rejection you encounter as a learning opportunity. What is it exactly about the work that wasn't right? Ask questions and be ready to look at your writing honestly and with as little emotion as possible.

Managing Your Time and Staying Disciplined

Don't know about you, but my mind keeps wandering at the moment, despite my best efforts to carry on finishing this book right now.

Yesterday I was meant to be finished with my first draft of this book, but I stumbled on an article about this new Dalgona coffee trend, and immediately had to try it myself. An hour later and I'd made a terrible, runny Dalgona, and the draft was consigned to "mañana".

Anyways, what I'm getting at is that procrastination is something most of us are *very* familiar with in our daily life. Think about it.

There are so many reasons to not feel motivated to get your work done. You might just not be feeling it that day. Everybody has those days and everybody needs those days sometimes. "I got this, but just not today". But when it's time to work it's time to work. Don't worry about motivation and don't worry about inspiration because discipline triumphs over them any day of the week. It's about having the discipline to get focused and write, no matter the distractions. And eventually that kind of discipline will become self perpetuating. You might even come to love the process.

I know that for me personally, I'm most disciplined and productive when I set a routine and try to stick with it as best as I can. Distractions are bound to happen though, so don't beat yourself up over it if you don't always stick to that routine. I've got kids at home, maybe some of you do too. To be happy around kids you kind of just have to embrace the chaos and enjoy yourself. Unfortunately, that kind of unpredictability isn't always schedule-friendly. No matter what your home situation is like, it's important to keep your expectations realistic and realize that a schedule isn't ever totally set in stone. Distractions will happen.

It's these kinds of distractions that can make managing your time challenging when working for yourself. If you have a boss or authority figure hovering over you. Getting things done becomes less of an issue because you know that there are tangible consequences to be felt. Don't feel like doing your job? That's fine— just don't expect to keep it long. For a freelancer, your client is like your boss in a certain respect, but really - you need to be the one running the show. That sounds easy in theory, but it can be somewhat difficult in practice.

There's nothing wrong with taking plenty of time for yourself to mentally and physically get in top shape. You need to be disciplined in those elements of your life too. And you also need to make sure that your relationships are all healthy— especially with your family.

But when it's time to write— you need to be focused on that as best you can.

But instead of cracking the whip on yourself like an authoritarian despot, be a good leader. If you're hard on yourself and don't get things done, you'll end up just feeling demoralized. What if you try a different approach? Don't be the uninspiring boss you hate, be the wise benevolent leader you'd love to have. Instead of punishing your mistakes, reward your achievements. You just spent 5 hours polishing up an amazing piece for a client? Time for a well deserved blunt break (or mango ice cream or whatever you like to reward yourself with).

Rewarding yourself can be a way to trick yourself into being more disciplined at first. Discipline will get you through when motivation is lacking.

To manage your time effectively, make sure to:

- Keep track of ALL due dates and time estimates for projects in Google Calendar or similar.
- Schedule specific time for each job.
- Work in time increments that work for your schedule.
- Manually or using an app, keep track of what you're spending your time on so you can improve.
- Set realistic expectations with clients.
- Experiment to learn what schedule works best for you and stick with.
- Focus your time on the activities that directly lead to the greatest measurable results.
- Use a timer (there are Google Doc add-ons for this)
- Know when to say no.

Let's drill into that last one some more.

The Power of The N Word

Effective management can be dumbed down to four words, *"learn to say NO"*. Setting priorities and learning to say no to yourself and the people and things around you is very important.

How often have you said yes to things to something that you later regretted? A bad relationship, time-consuming personal obligations, overwhelming requests from your boss? By saying no to things that get in the way of your ability to do what you need to do, you can have the power to make those issues disappear. Doing this will also help you gain a stronger sense of what's really important for you in your life. You'll be freed to say yes to the things in your life that really open the door to abundance and happiness.

10 Ways For Writers to Improve Focus

As important as it is to manage your time properly and learn to say no, sometimes finding the focus to write can be equally challenging. Writers often think they don't have enough time, when the real issue is they lack focus. Here are ten ways to improve focus for writers:

1. Remove Distractions

You sit down to write and next thing you know, you find yourself cleaning up the kitchen or distracted by some other chore around the house. Then without realizing it you've been on social media for fifteen minutes. Before you know it, the whole day can get away from you with this kind of stuff. Intentionally limiting distractions can be an excellent way to focus more effectively. Easier said than done, but the idea is to go around the house and get rid of anything that's distracting you. Pay the bills, make the kids breakfast, clean the toilet, Marie Kondo your belongings so everything sparks joy— do the whole nine yards. Sometimes though, that stuff just needs to wait. Sometimes working from home is just naturally distracting. It's unavoidable. Particularly if you have kids or pets. If your situation allows for it, you might want to simply go somewhere else to get your work done. Maybe a library, a coffee shop, or a coworking space. Alternatively, you may be able to find a small space in your home where you can self-isolate and keep distractions to a minimum. My family and I live in South Florida and attached to our home we have this tiny room with rickety walls and no air conditioning. I write there most of the time, because it's far too hot for my noisey (wonderful!) kids to stand. Sometimes you've got to suffer a little to avoid distractions.

2. Try Meditation

If you research the daily habits of some of the worlds most successful individuals, you'll find that many of them engage in some form of daily meditation. The word meditation means different things to different people, but at its core it is remarkably simple. For those not familiar, meditation is a habit of training your mind to focus and redirect your thoughts. One aspect of meditating is learning to note thoughts that arise without attaching to them. Part of the aim is to focus and redirect your thoughts to increase awareness of yourself and your surroundings. This can all tend to sound a little abstract. Honestly, don't be intimidated— you don't need to sit there cross legged for hours at a time. It can be as simple as you laying down on the ground with your eyes closed counting your breaths for a minute. One breathe in, two breathe out. One breathe in, two breathe out, etc. As you get more into it you may find you'll want to do it longer and longer (that's what she said), but start easy and set your expectations low at first (ha!). It takes time to find your groove while meditating. Also remember, there's no wrong way to do it. You can meditate when you're in line at the grocery store or while doing dishes - it doesn't need to be some elaborate ordeal. It isn't necessary to meditate immediately before you write to get a benefit out of this either. You'll still find it helpful no matter when you find the time to squeeze it in.

3. Break Out The Jams

One of the first things on my daily routine in the morning is to put on some music. If I forget to do this, everything will seem to go wrong. Only I won't necessarily notice it for an hour or so. Then— of course, no music! That's what was wrong, no wonder why things weren't flowing. What you are hearing (or not hearing) when you're trying to write can have a big effect on your focus. If music's not your personal style, you might also try noise cancelling headphones, earplugs, or even white noise apps to help you get focused.

4. Clear Your Head With A Freewriting Session

Some writers find it useful to start off their writing session with five to fifteen minutes of freewriting. One idea behind doing this is that you can dump out any negative thoughts or emotions that may tend to block your writing. What you write during these sessions doesn't necessarily need to be related to what you'll be writing for that day. You're just trying to get rid of any distractions. They might be thoughts of family issues, relationships, your job, or even the writing you're doing. A short freewriting session can often help to contemplate things and bring clarity to your day.

5. Intentionally Limit Your Writing Sessions

On the surface this seems like an awful idea. You don't need less time to write, you need more. The thing is, you might be giving yourself so much time that the brain thinks it's okay to start wasting time. That natural inclination to dawdle is just going to be worse if you brain knows you have lots of time available. It's something that's happened to a lot of writers. They finally take the plunge and try to write full-time, only to find they spend much of their day procrastinating. Somehow they manage to get even less done than when they had more time. As a father who writes from home I can tell you that you will almost certainly have razor-sharp focus after having children. Your time simply because so limited that you're forced to seize whatever free moments you possibly can and make them work. If you find your focus starts to drift, try cutting back on the length of your writing sessions to see how it works for you.

6. Plan Ahead

A lot of writers do mental work outside of their regular writing session. Remember when I mentioned that you should carry a notepad or a note taking app? This is why. You never know when you're going to come up with the perfect outline for your clients article. If you're able to do planning work during free moments throughout the day, you'll be free to really focus on writing when the time comes. Keeping your project in mind during different parts of the day may sound like an awful overstep of the whole work/life balance thing, but honestly to me personally I feel like the technique saves me time and reduces stress overall. It makes it feel like less of a mental shift when it's time to sit down and write. If you're comfortable doing some planning outside of your regular writing sessions, give this technique a try. You might also try combining this with the shortened writing sessions described above to see if your focus is helped.

7. Avoid Distractions on The Internet

The internet is a tool with limitless potential for writers. It's a limitless repository of humankind's knowledge, as well as a limitless opportunity to waste your time. You can connect with writers and clients everywhere on the planet, or you can watch some *spectacular* cat videos all day. Maybe you think you're just hopping on a social site for a split second, but before you know it your whole day is gone and your project is behind schedule. If you can, it's best to avoid looking up facts or doing research during a writing session. Websites are specifically made to suck you in for as long as possible— that's how they get paid. To avoid their allure, some writers simply turn off their wifi or work somewhere without internet. Likewise, they keep their phones and tablets out of reach as well. Of course, you could also write with a good old fashioned pencil and paper. There may be some drawbacks to writing with pen or pencil, but it can be a fantastic way to keep focused while writing.

A last option to limit internet distractions is to use apps and extensions for your browser that will prevent you from spending too much time on time-wasting sites. You set your browsing limitations based on your exact needs, so it can be a great way to actively deter your browsing urges.

8. Use The Pomodoro Technique

The Pomodoro technique is a popular approach to creativity that is highly adaptable. With this technique, all of your tasks are broken down into 25-minute periods (referred to as Pomodoros) with a 3-5 minute break between each Pomodoro. There is also a longer break after every four Pomodoros. This method encourages short bursts of focus and productivity, and can rely on a ticking and ringing timer to encourage walking and resting. There's more to it than this, but if it sounds like something that would work for you please check this technique out. Many very prolific entrepreneurs and creatives also divide their day into set increments of one length of time or another for the sake of efficiency. Elon Musk famously schedules his day into 5 minute segments.

9. Get Physically Active

You don't need to run marathons to get benefit from regular physical activity. Low impact activities such as walking or swimming can greatly help you stay more focused, relieve stress, and benefit your overall health. Regular exercise also helps with sleeping, which is something your brain will need plenty of in order to write.

10. Herbal Focus Remedies

I'm sure you can guess one possible herbal remedy that might help focus here. The right Sativa strain might be perfect to help you focus. Or maybe for your body chemistry a hybrid will have a better effect on your ability to focus. There are, of course, many other substances you could try to help you focus— from chamomile to adderall. I'm not going to get into all those, but I do think that it's worth investigating anything that's healthy for you and truly helps you focus.

We all struggle to focus sometimes. It's ultimately something that all writers have to deal with in a way that works best for them. There may be times when some approaches work better than others for you, so experiment with different tools and be open to trying new ways to improve your focus.

Always Read Everything Out Loud

This is probably one of the most understated habits of successful writers. If you want to have an accurate idea of the image that your copy projects, you must read your writing out loud.

When it comes to doing quality writing that hits home, reading it aloud is one of the surest ways to evaluate your words. You should do this fresh—read it out to yourself after the copy has been finished and you've taken a mandatory 'rest' away from the work.

Personally, I mostly work in Google Docs for my word processing. What I like to do is use a Chrome extension to read my text aloud to me. That way I can pretty much relax there with some tea and have my words read back to me while I closely listen for mistakes. This isn't a foolproof method—there will be mistakes you don't catch and so you'll still need to manually read it over.

The Importance of Reading

To most freelancers, the daily grind is to get a job, deliver, get paid. There's a temptation to spend every hour you can hustling and writing to make as much money as you can. But don't do it! This will inevitably lead to burnout and you giving up altogether.

Instead, make sure you dedicate ample time to reading. Ideally every day.

As Stephen King says, "If you don't have time to read, you don't have the time (or the tools) to write. Simple as that.". He's an incredibly prolific writer who's been incredibly successful— so if he can find time to read *and* write, so can you. It doesn't have to be for a long time each day and it can easily be during mundane things like waiting in line at the grocery store. It's easier than ever to have amazing reading material on you 24/7 so there's really no excuse.

Check on your phone how much time you spend each day on apps like YouTube and Instagram and realize that you could probably use some of that time more productively by reading. Or listening to audio books or podcasts - maybe even ones about getting better at writing!

Notably, reading not only improves your vocabulary, but it also develops you into a better thinker, helps build people skills, strengthens analytical skills, and it improves your mental health.

Write Conversationally

There's a time and place for big words and complex writing. Medically-oriented cannabis writing, for instance. Generally speaking though, you'll be better off writing the way people actually speak. You'll tend to pull in a wider audience that way. Nobody's saying to write poorly, but at the same time you want to write honestly and authentically. It's a fine line to walk, but here are a few tips:

- When writing, imagine that you are in a conversation with someone. Talk to that person as you would with a real person. Let the conversation play out in your head as you write. Would you feel weird saying the things you're writing?

- Write with a purpose: I am writing to educate and inspire you to become a cannabis food writer, cannabis application writer, cannabis freelance writer, etc. that's my purpose, what's yours?

- Don't be a smartass: what if the reader doesn't get your joke? What if your writing comes off as pretentious or too formal or difficult to read? It means lost audience and a high bounce rate. Keep your work simple, friendly, useful and relatable.

- Speak your writing aloud: There's no faster way to realize how needlessly wordy something is than by reading it.

A big part of making your writing more conversational has to do with the readability of the writing. One way to test for readability is to... read it. Reading it aloud you will easily spot any issues with flow, pacing, or anything related to readability. Another option is to test your content with real people. For example, reach out to family, friends, or colleagues, and have them assess your writing. Ask them if they have any suggestions about making it more readable. If you're still struggling, you can also find a number of different Chrome extensions and other software that are designed to help writers grow their skills.

Writing to be Virally Spread

It's impossible to predict what piece of content will take off and go viral, but there are a few things you can do to maximize the chances of your writing being shared.

A study done by Johan Berger and Katherine L. Milkman and published in the Journal of Marketing Research found emotionality, positivity, awe, anger, anxiety, and sadness to be the primary predictors of viral content. Meaning, if you target the right emotions with your writing, your writing could give your audience something to talk about. If they want to talk about it, maybe they'll share it with their connections on social media sites. And if they do that, it stands a better chance of going viral. That's because your work targets them on a personal level.

For example, "Why is Cannabis So Damn Expensive?" is an article that was published in LA Weekly a few years back. Now, what cannabis-loving human among us has not asked this question at least once in our lives? It's a personally relatable feeling. And the title basically promises that it has the answer to that question. That's why it strikes a chord and maybe it'll entice you to read and share.

Recently, Buzzsumo analyzed 100 million posts, the found that articles that go viral share some similarities or characteristics:

- Viral articles are ones that invoke laughter, awe or amusement and appeal to people's narcissistic side.
- Long-form content gets more social shares than short-form content.
- Having images in your posts leads to more social media shares.
- 'Lists of 10' get four times as many social shares as other lists.
- People tend to share content that looks trustworthy.
- Social media Influencers get you more retweets and shares.
- Old content should be re-promoted on a regular basis.
- The best day to publish new content is Tuesday.

It's also worth noting that positive emotional content goes viral faster than negative emotional content. Although admittedly, it might not always feel that way.

Engaging Emotion Through Copywriting

Sales copywriting involves communicating your message or solution in the most effective way possible. With *emotion* being a critical component of the buyer's psyche, it makes perfect sense you should write sales copy that focuses on eliciting an emotional response. Sales copy that addresses specific human emotions, like fear and pain, will be easily relatable to buyers that believe you have the answer to their desires.

Using engaging words and stories will help the reader better identify with your message and create a significant impression for the ultimate purpose of conversion. A successful sales copywriter looks to capture the audience's imagination with evocative words that are designed to elicit an emotional response. And hopefully, if the copy is good enough, the reader may feel drawn to your client's product or service.

Writing Effective Product Descriptions

Aside from photos, product descriptions often serve as a product's "first impression". Because of this, descriptions are critical to the sale. With so many new products being rolled out each year, there's virtually never ending demand for great product descriptions. Descriptions can be a lucrative source of an income for writers in the cannabis space, so they're something that's worth getting good at..

Fantastic product descriptions are an essential component in building a brand that appeals to buyers. The descriptions need to be written in a voice that matches the brand while at the same time listing all the important details of the item. It's crucial that all the actual references to the product be 100% accurate, or you could cause trouble for the company down the road.

Make sure that product descriptions are optimized to include any pertinent keywords that the brand is trying to target for that particular product. By targeting the right keywords that customers are searching for, copywriters can position their clients' content to achieve the highest possible conversions.

While keyword-stuffing remains terrible and dated practice, infusing well written content with appropriately descriptive keywords will absolutely benefit your client's search engine ranking.

Provide Solutions With Stories

Storytelling has proven to be an effective medium for securing the attention of potential customers while delivering your message in a subtle manner.

Successful sales writers have honed the ability to use storytelling in presenting the unique solutions and benefits offered by a product to prospects. All this while forming an emotional connection with the reader to, hopefully, make the sale.

Testimonials, case studies, and brand stories are good sources of usable material in creating captivating stories that readers can connect with. Storytelling also offers skilled copywriters a not-so-obvious avenue for utilizing keyword-rich text that should perform well in organic search results.

Demand attention immediately

"Either write something worth reading or do something worth writing", said Benjamin Franklin. He was pointing to the fact that we don't write for the hell of it. We write to be read and ultimately to get paid.You want clients to flock to you and you want people to discuss the things you write about.

What you need to realize is people are constantly bombarded by so much content every second of their day. They may have mere seconds to devote to your writing. For that reason, you must make each word count and write with intention!

Build Curiosity

Have you noticed a gap between what you know about cannabis and what you want to know?

Psychologists call this the "curiosity gap". This feeling is normally triggered through writing by providing tiny bits of information that bully the reader into wanting to find out more.

Information presented is very limited. They give you the general idea but they don't go into specifics. The trick is to give your readers incomplete, intriguing information without giving your story or argument away.

Improve Upon Ideas - Never Plagiarize

Plagiarism is a form of theft. You are benefiting from someone else's hard work. It goes without saying that you should never use other people's writing and try to pass it off as your own. It will kill your credibility and trustworthiness in the long run.

That being said, there is nothing wrong with approaching the same topic as someone else's has and writing it from your own perspective. Two authors can be given the same topic to write about and even the same basic outline of what they're going to cover and still create very different writing.

In essence, what I am telling you is, when you are out of ideas, don't be fearful of taking inspiration from writing styles and topics that you like. It could help you to bring in fresh ideas that you might otherwise not have considered.

Make Your Content Scannable

As humans, we are hardwired to scan for information. Because of that, you should format your posts in a way that it's easy for the reader to scan.

What makes an article scannable?

- Short paragraphs and sentences
- Subheadings (H1, H2, H3)
- Bullet points (like these)

How to Write Attention-Grabbing Cannabis Headlines

8 out of 10 visitors won't read past your headline, so headlines can literally make or break your content strategy. Here's everything you need to write successful cannabis blog headlines, with examples to help you get started.

When a headline is done right, it can change the way people read content and the way they remember it. Sometimes it even becomes a gateway to a discussion that will be debated for years to come.

"The Problem with the Current High Potency THC Marijuana" and "Is Marijuana as Safe as We Think?" are examples of headlines done right! Mention either of these headlines and chances are you will find yourself in a deep discussion or argument over the pros and cons of marijuana use. That's where the power of headlines lies— their ability to fuel debate and spark interest on a subject matter makes headlines a vital part of writing.

Although writing headlines may feel like a small task, stringing together short sets of words can have very big implications on the way the reader views the world. This makes your headline the key determinant of whether your content is being found and consumed or not.

A great headline must do two things: It has to engage your audience or reader; and, at the same time, send signals to search engines that help rank content. Professionals don't create headlines for the sake of it—they create authentic, quality headlines and content that audiences want to share.

Here's everything you need to know about building successful cannabis blog headlines, with examples to help you get started.

Headline Element 1: Trigger Your Audience's Emotions With The Right Words

"A Sexual Health Expert Explains Why Weed is Great for the Bedroom"

Vs

"Reasons Why Weed is Great for Sex"

In your opinion, which of the two is the superior headline? Don't peak, just say out loud which headline is more clickable than the other with a specific reason.

With Valentine's Day just a few days ahead as I write this, both headlines seem like logical options for a post. However, the first headline has more charisma than the second. Why do I say that?

Right off the bat, the first headline establishes authority. 'A Sexual Health Expert' is someone with knowledge of how intercourse works. Because of that, his or her opinions are not only reliable, they are also trustworthy.

The second headline is lazy and uninspired. Yes, it can work; but it won't rank better on search engine indexes or generate as many clicks as the first one. To make an effective cannabis-related headline, you must include key trigger words that are relevant to your audience.

What Are Trigger Words?

Generally speaking, "trigger words" are short and precise words that are packed with emotion. These are words like 'how-to,' 'overcome,' 'why or how,' 'amazing,' and so on.

Trigger words are important in headlines in that they make the reader feel something. Like in this case *why weed is great for the bedroom"*, wants you to experience sexual emotions as you read the article and try out the recommendations afterward.

Notice something? This type of headline goes beyond reading. It places a foothold in your thoughts that helps you retain information. In other words, you won't forget the article as soon as you read it. That means that even if you forget the content you will always remember the headline and the general ideas it represents, and that will keep you coming back.

What should a headline look like?

- Longer headlines tell a better story and increase engagement.
- Limited use of positive sentiments builds curiosity.

Some Examples

- No Rolling Paper? No Problem? - Top Hacks When You Run Out of Smoking Papers
- Is Your Rolling Paper Safe? Top 10 Safe Alternatives to Rolling Paper
- No Rolling Papers? How to Smoke Weed Without Rolling Paper
- Cannabis DIY Hacks - How to Roll a Toilet Paper Joint and Oher Genius Ideas

This brings us to the second and most important element of great marijuana headlines, curiosity!

Headline Element 2: Curiosity Is King

Why do humans do stuff? A simple question with a simple answer: Curiosity!

You started smoking weed because of curiosity, you chose to read this article out of curiosity, and our species continues to thrive because of it. If you want to get someone to read your content, you must make him or her curious.

Question: What makes us curious?

Curiosity is driven by two things; it is driven by:

1. Something that doesn't quite agree with what we know or think we know—something that surprises us.
2. Pleasure.

We all know that smoking weed gets you high. But a new user has questions like: *"Will it affect my driving?"*, *"Will weed kill my motivation?"*, *"What do you do when you get too high?"*, and so on. You want to tease your audience while at the same time withholding what that information actually is.

The truth of the matter is a huge chunk of the human population are lazy readers. Most of us skim through content. A good headline will build curiosity; however, if you don't answer the question in the first half of your article, then most people won't keep reading. That's where the F-pattern comes in.

The F-pattern or format is where the writer includes the most important points in the first two paragraphs and uses subheadings generously throughout to make reading fast and easy. The trick is to make sure that each paragraph perfectly transitions into the next. You answer the first question, but you create more curiosity by asking another related question.

Example Headlines That Build Curiosity

A curiosity-building headline is one that captures your reader's attention. Here is an example:

"Are You Wasting Weed? Tips for Conserving Weed and Still Getting High"

Notice that this headline has several layers of curiosity.

1. First, it asks you a question you may already be asking yourself.
2. Second, it promises to show you how to conserve your weed and still have a good time.

The headline could have read something generic like, *How to Stop Wasting Weed.* But that's boring and overused.

Headline Element 3: Always Offer Value

We are all looking for something. It could be a good laugh, answers to an itching question, a little pick-me-up, or it could be advice. To your reader, the answers you give or satisfying a need he or she has is valuable.

Let's say a user wants to find a good playlist to listen to while high. If you compile a playlist that the user finds satisfactory while high, then you have provided them something of value. However, you can't provide value if you don't know what you are writing about. For that reason, you should know your shit before you publish.

So don't just start writing or posting without any forethought. Think first about your audience: What do they like? What are their experiences like? Then think about what you can do to improve their lives a little.

The Problem With Value

Value is very subjective. There is no physical right or wrong, and you can't touch it. Instead, it's about giving your audience practical and useful information that they can use in real life.

Here are some examples:

- The Ultimate Guide to Cannabinoids and Cannabis
- Top 10/20 Health/Medical Benefits of Marijuana
- Health Benefits of Medical Marijuana
- What is the Difference Between Regular Marijuana and Medical Marijuana?

Expert Tip: Optimize Your Native Ad Headlines To Trigger Associations

What do I mean? A native ad is simply an ad that doesn't look like an ad; instead, they blend into the editorial flow of the social media or web page you are on. This is where phrases like "suggested posts" and "promoted posts" come in. These phrases tie in the ads with the content the reader is already interested in, encouraging the reader to click them.

Remember, most of your audience is consuming your content on mobile devices and some have ad blockers. The advantage of using native ads is they command more focus and attention and they allow you to tell stories in a non-annoying way to highly distracted mobile users.

Headline Element 4: Say Something Shocking!

"10 Benefits of Using Marijuana, NUMBER 3 WILL SHOCK YOU AND YOUR MUM!"

Vs.

"Researchers Claim Cannabis Use Increases the Risk of Psychosis—Just as New York Liberalizes Marijuana Laws"

Which of these two is the better headline?

If you are new to the internet, then you may not have noticed that the first headline is obvious clickbait. The second headline, on the other hand, digs deep into your paranoia. It says, *"Wait a minute... What if there ARE health dangers associated with cannabis use!?"* That's why it works so well. The second headline also suggests expertise and authority to the reader by including words like 'researchers' and 'laws.'

In the right hands, clickbait can work, but it will only attract first-time audiences. The problem here is once they have read through your BS, they won't have any reason to come back. In fact, you've likely turned them off to your future content as well.

The idea is to tell your audience something that will have a personal effect on them, possibly immediately. There are two ways to do this: Either let the shocking information linger, stringing the reader along; or pick it up immediately in the first paragraph of your content.

Personally, I follow eight little steps (not necessarily in any order):

1. Make a provocative statement that incites curiosity or shocks your audience.
2. Tell a story.
3. Be authentic—write content that feels close to home (something relatable).
4. Quote influential people or trustworthy sources to solidify your arguments.
5. Use visual aids to spice up your content.
6. Ask questions to engage your audience.
7. Tell a joke to keep the reader entertained.
8. Use phrases like 'imagine' or 'think of this' to get your reader thinking (the longer they think the longer they stay on your site or page).

Headline Element 5: Speak Directly To Your Audience

If you run a cannabis business, then your business is to talk to people who use cannabis, people who are curious about cannabis, or people who want to profit from it. And the right way to talk to your audience is to get at them directly. By that I mean, you should use direct language.

What is direct language? Notice that throughout this article I have used words like 'you' and 'your.' I could have generalized and used indirect words like 'them' to address you, but using words like 'you' makes the reader feel like you are talking directly to him/her.

Here are some examples of direct headlines

- Everything You Should Know About Vaping Cannabis
- The 10 High-THC Strains You Should Know About
- The Best Cannabis Strains For Your Workout
- Everything You Should Know About Medical Cannabis

Why does it work? Direct statements give off the impression that you are a clear thinker; they also show that the writer is a human being. That's important because when you're reading the headline or post, it feels like a conversation is happening in your brain.

The trick is to frame your purpose by stating your intention very early in the conversation or writing. Don't try to be smarter or appear better educated or cooler than your reader or audience. Instead, put yourself in their shoes. Ask yourself questions like, "What questions do I need answered?"

All in all, the best pieces of advice I can give you here are: Be yourself; speak from your own experiences; and, when given the choice, choose simpler language.

Headline Element 6: Include Numbers (Our Brains Are Hard-Wired To Love Lists)

"20 Reasons to Stay Away from Weed"
On the surface, this headline sounds unprofessional, clickbait-y, and it possibly feels like you've seen a variation of it somewhere.

However, if you look around, then you will notice that the internet is littered with 'Top' lists. Why is that?

Writer and philosopher Umberto Eco once said, "We like lists because we don't want to die." He added, "How, as a human being, does one face infinity? How does one attempt to grasp the incomprehensible?" Well, it's simple really; we create lists!

What he is really saying is: We love lists because they enable us to digest information in bite-sized form. Let me clarify. If I click on *"10 Ways to Hide Weed from the Cops"*, then I know exactly what I am going to get. This type of headline is clear, to the point, and focused on value. But (and this is a huge BUT!) you will only impress the reader if the sub-headlines are appropriate and work in tandem with the main headline.

How do you do it? It is important to realize that the most popular Google searches are ones that help the reader solve a specific problem. For example, a title like *"20 Reasons to Stay Away from Weed"*, sets up the reader to expect negative consequences associated with weed. It shocks and plays with your expectations, making it irresistible to some.

The Element of Trust

Ever read something and felt like the writer was reading your mind? That's how experienced writers establish trust.

If a headline promises something, then, as the writer, you must make sure that you deliver on that promise. For example, if your headline promises, *"10 Unique Ways to Smoke Weed Without Rolling Paper"*, then make sure that you deliver 10 arguments. And, of course, the general idea is to back up your promise with compelling or useful information.

Cannabis is a very hands-on subject; by that, I mean, you can't write about cannabis experiences without ever having used weed in the first place. And that's where many businesses get it wrong. For example, if you have never smoked weed out of an orange, potato, or apple, then don't write about smoking weed out of any of those fruits (unless if it's an opinion piece).

Why? You don't know the challenges; you don't know the upsides; and your information might end up misleading your audience. All of that will break trust.

Researchers have found that <u>headlines with numbers generate more than 70% social shares and engagement</u>. Think about it, *"20 Ways to Make Smoking Weed More Delightful"* sounds way better than *"Ways to Make Smoking Weed More Delightful"*, doesn't it?

Here are some examples to get you started:

- 20 Ways to Make Smoking Weed More Delightful
- 10 Marijuana Strains that Will Make You Feel Better About the World
- 12 Harsh Truths About Weed that Will Make You Think

Notice *"...Will Make You..."*. On social media, this phrase, according to Steven Rayson from <u>BuzzSumo</u>, gains more than twice the number of Facebook engagements as the second most popular headline phrase. They came to that conclusion after analyzing 100 million headlines on the internet.

Headline Element 7: Play With Their Emotions And Expectations

"Are You Working Harder than Ever? Here Are 5 Marijuana Strains to Help You Relax"

What emotional benefit can you see in the headline above? On my part, I can see that this headline wants you to feel in control of your life. It acknowledges the fact that you work hard and promises to help you find ways to take off the edge.

Just like you, your reader or customer is a human being. For that reason, he or she is sometimes sad, anxious, joyful, afraid, empathetic, bored, confused, and so on. Let's assume that you woke up sad or depressed today for whatever reason. If you see a headline like, *"Why People Smoke Weed to Treat Depression"*, then it is highly likely that you will click on that headline. Why?

Sadness and depression are not positive feelings. Some people believe (including myself) that as a species we are hard-wired to want to be happy. If something promises you joy, you are drawn to it. It is in your nature. This is where words like 'what', 'when', 'where', and 'why' come in.

Your readers' emotions are caused by his or her thoughts on a subject or situation. Therefore, if we are in the same situation, then we might experience very different sets of emotions. So, you have to define the what, when, why and where in your headlines.

How Do You Spark Emotions?

Paint a picture in your readers' head. By that I mean, answer the what, why, when and where questions. Doing that makes your headlines feel like they are grounded in reality. For example, *"What to Use When You Have No Rolling Paper"*. The 'when' in that headline refers to a relatable situation where your reader has marijuana but no way of smoking it.

Here are some more examples:

- You Are Running Out of Weed! What Should You Do Next?
- Here's What You Need to Know About CBD Products that Could Hurt Your Pet

What your headline has to do is make your reader feel special, angry, or any emotion at all. If he or she feels it, then the headline becomes more relatable, thus more clickable. For example, *"Here's What You Need to Know About CBD Products that Could Hurt Your Pet"*.

Humans, at least most of them, love their pets. Consequently, if you tell someone something that directly affects what they personally care about, then most of them will feel the urgency or need to get that information. Sneaky, I know, but it works too well to be ignored.

Generally speaking, to properly sell your headlines via emotions you should:

1. First, figure out which emotion has the right appeal to your audience. (This could be things like greed, fear, altruism, envy, pride, or shame.)

2. Use the right words in your headline.
3. Help your readers realize the cost of inaction and emphasize on the personal consequences and benefits.
4. Tell them what they have to lose.

Pride and envy. These are the hardest emotions to work with, but that doesn't mean that it's impossible. One way of using these emotions is to show the reader what they are missing out on.

Here are some examples:

- 30 Celebrities Who Smoke Weed
- Top 5 Celebrity Potheads
- Famous Weed Smokers in History

This begs the question, "If 'they' are doing it and they are successful, then why don't I?"

Headline Element 8: The Power Of "How-To"

Being human is in itself a 'how-to experience.' Think about it. We all want to learn how to do stuff. That's why we go to school, and that's why we ask questions.

Almost all writers are guilty of using 'how-to' in a headline, and there is good reason for that. The reason why readers love clicking on this type of headline is that they are clear, specific, detailed, and value based.

"How-To" headlines are ultra-specific, meaning that readers know exactly what to expect when they click. However, experts, such as Neil Patel, recommend that you avoid basic adjectives, such as 'complete.' Instead, spice up your headlines with exciting words such as 'exhilarating,' 'provoke,' 'insane,' 'crazy,' or anything else that works.

How To Appeal To Your Readers' "How-To" Instincts

As a person, you want to improve both your personal and financial life, right? The same is true with the person reading your content. As a consequence of that, you as the writer have to focus on the end results. Take a step back, try to figure out what problems your readers are currently struggling with, then narrow down these problems to a very specific question.

An easy way to do this is to check comments or visit sites like Reddit or Cannabis Forums and look at the questions being asked. The idea is to position yourself as a problem solver. You want to be a voice of authority! Remember, how-to articles at their core promise to teach someone how to do something. DO THAT!

Pro tip: Be specific, don't generalize.
Here are some examples:

- How to Grow Weed Like a Pro: The Ultimate Guide
- How to Travel with Weed and Not Get Caught
- How to Roll the Perfect Joint Filter—Every Time
- How to Roll a Joint
- How to Start a Marijuana Business and Get Paid

Headline Element 9: Create A Sense Of Urgency

Have you ever noticed that you feel under pressure when you have less time and more to do? With millions, if not billions, of articles published every day, the average internet user has lots of options. What he or she doesn't have is time.

For this to work, your headline must be Unique, Useful, Ultra-specific, and Urgent. I'm sure you can figure out the first three U's; the problem for most writers is 'urgent.' You want your audience to feel or think that they are missing out on something. What am I talking about?

"Marijuana Use Is Rising Among Young Adults—Especially College Students—Study Shows"

That headline I copied from CNN creates a sense of urgency in that it presents a problem that we have to speak about now. College students smoking weed is a concern for parents, because most of them are unaware of the consequences. Another good example of this type of headline is this:

"Nearly 66,000 Marijuana Convictions in Los Angeles County Will Be Dismissed, District Attorney Says"

People in jail or prison over marijuana-related cases or people related to them will feel the need to read that article. They want to know when these new measures are coming into place and how it will affect them.

You want the reader to think that he or she needs the information you have right now! Not tomorrow, not in a few months, but right now!

Here are some more examples

- How-To Stop Wasting Weed Right Now
- Marijuana: Important Things to Know
- How-To Talk About Marijuana with Your Son or Daughter

The Zeigarnik Effect

Ever noticed that when you start working on something but fail to finish it that thoughts of the unfinished work follow you around like a bad stench? These types of thoughts push you into going back and finishing what you started. Discovered by Bluma Zeigarnik, the Zeigarnik effect is based on experiments carried out in the 1920s that are still relevant today.

What is it? The simplest way I can think of to describe this effect is as a 'cliffhanger' or an 'unanswered question.' To write better headlines, you need to use this effect to create unease in your target audience.

For example:

- "Want to Double Your Indoor Marijuana Yield But Don't Have Space? Find Out How"
- "Make $4,000/per Month Testing Weed At Home"

These types of headlines are best used in ads. They are great in that they leave your audience literally hanging. It's like telling someone an incomplete story prompting him or her to ask you to give more details.

However, there is a difference between teasing your audience and straight-up lying to them. Lying is a huge NO-NO because it breaks trust. For that reason, never deceive your audience—the promise you make has to pay off in some way.

Headline Element 10: Get Statistical

"Did You Know that Over 75% of People on the Planet Have Admitted to Using Cannabis at Least Once?"

How true is this statement? The truth is, I just made it up; but, if I didn't tell you that, then you'd still believe me. Why? The problem with most of us is that we don't understand the potential causes for bias during data collection, the assumptions, and the ins and outs. All we get are the numbers.

Numbers make the reader feel like he or she is getting something worthwhile. These types of headlines grab attention because they show that you (the writer) not only know your stuff, but you also get your information from reliable sources.

It goes without saying that dropping in statistics that are relevant to your market is of the utmost importance. Whether we can or cannot trust statistical data is a whole other conversation in itself; however, you can use statistics to your advantage when creating headlines. How is that?

"Canada just Gave Fathers 8-Months of Paid Leave While 90% of Americans Still Get Zero"

What's special about this headline is how simple and effective it is at driving its message. It shows a contrast between two places, thus expanding the scope of its reach, and it uses statistics to show the difference. These types of headlines release a small amount of information to pique curiosity and prime your hunger for knowledge. That's why they work so well.

Here are some examples:

- 76% of Doctors Are in Favor of Using Marijuana for Medical Purposes: Here Is Why
- 92% of Patients Say Marijuana Can Relieve Symptoms Associated with HIV, AIDS, Alzheimer's, and Cancer, According to a New Report
- 51% of Americans Favor Marijuana Legalization: Learn Why

The Upworthy Formula

Although not a marijuana-based business, Upworthy is a website that has perfected the art of writing headlines. The writers there follow a very simple yet effective formula.

Most of the headlines you'll find on Upworthy signify a story of a video showing or describing an injustice. These are not your typical social justice warrior headlines; instead, they have very well thought out stories that most of us can relate to. For example:

- "Seth Rogen and Evan Goldberg Are Making a Serious Push to Expunge Peoples' Pot Convictions"
- "Mother of Two Takes a Bold Stance By Proudly Proclaiming that Weed Makes Her a 'Better Mom'"

Notice how simple and to the point Upworthy headlines are. If you are a mother and you smoke weed or are curious about it, then you will find it difficult to resist clicking on the second headline. Why? Because it's relatable, and it promises to deliver on something that is of interest to you.

The other headline, though it doesn't feel like it, is a push against the injustice committed by the authorities against people who have been charged for marijuana-related crimes. It promises to inspire or amaze the reader into some form of action.

Another thing you may have noticed is the type of visuals they use. Scattered throughout each article, no matter how serious or light-hearted the issue is, there are lots of visual aids. Unlike traditional websites that use stock images only, Upworthy articles also include memes and gifs.

Generally speaking, Upworthy writes for people, and so should you. Here are some examples of how:

- Use classic attractors such as celebrities, sex, and miracle cures in your headlines.
- Be creative with your headlines—don't feel squeezed by traditional boundaries.
- Put odd and interesting things in your headlines to build curiosity.
- Tell a story through your headlines

How To Perfect The Upworthy Formula:

Tell stories that hit close to home, and give your audience something they can relate to.

- "A Neighborhood Mom Thought She Caught Her Teen Babysitter Smoking and Was Hilariously Wrong"

1. Inspire or give your audience hope for a better future.
   "Marijuana-based Medicine Has Been Approved By the FDA—It's a Sign of Hope"

2. Call out 'The Man' or speak about an injustice that might be affecting your audience.

- "Body-cam Images Appear to Show Police Planting Weed On a Black Teenager. What Do You See?"

How To Craft Killer Cannabis Headlines: A Summary

Multiple studies have found that "number headlines" are more effective than any other type of headline. If you check sites like

BuzzFeed, you will notice that most of their headlines are either numbers headlines or headlines that address readers.

"Is that it? Should I only use numbers and reader-addressing headlines?" you ask. Even if you follow all the rules, three questions still remain.

1.   What is the point of your article or video?
2.   How does it benefit me as the reader?
3.   If I was looking for this, what would I Google?

"What would I Google?" is the most important question you should ask yourself when writing a headline. Let me ask you a simple question. If you were Google and a fire broke out in New York, which report would you rank higher in your search index? Is it one by the BBC or the New York Times? Obviously, the report by the New York times will rank higher. Why? They are closer to the information, and can thus tell a better story. It's all about relevance!

And ask yourself these questions each time you start writing a headline. "How relevant is it to my audience?" "What are people searching for in search engines?" There are lots of tools, including Alexa and SEMrush, that can help you answer these questions. Use them! And stay relevant.

You also have to think about how Google algorithms personalize news and content for its users. For example, if I have a history of searching for cute kittens, then Google will recommend similar stories to me. This makes it very important to find out what your audience is searching for and what's currently happening in the industry.

www.ingramcontent.com/pod-product-compliance
Lightning Source LLC
Chambersburg PA
CBHW031252250726
48655CB00005B/2184